Michael Frayn
Plays: 3

Here, Now You Know, La Belle Vivette

Here: Quirky, clever, teasing . . . one of the theatre's subtlest, most sophisticated minds.' *The Times*

'Frayn's excellent new play . . . is primarily a play of ideas . . . The action is tightly patterned, the language highly (and wittily) styled. At the same time there are realistic lessons to be learned.' *Sunday Telegraph*

Now You Know: 'Frayn has come up with a new play that puts one in mind of *The Wild Duck*: a fascinating and highly intelligent look at the problems of being totally open in a secretive society . . . a teasing moral comedy that puts dramatic flesh on the eternal dilemmas.' *Guardian*

'. . . is what Frayn does brilliantly and best: the gentle revelation that people, like organisations, are totally unable to realise the very objectives they have worthily chosen for themselves . . . the most enjoyable comedy in town, a stylish little masterpiece of minute social and political observation. Nobody does this better than Frayn.' *Spectator*

La Belle Vivette: 'Immensely entertaining: intelligent, articulate, ingenious, a welcome relief after some of the ghastliness Offenbach is subjected to.' *Time Out*

'Frayn should be congratulated.' *Daily Telegraph*

Michael Frayn was born in London in 1933 and began his career as a journalist on the *Guardian* and the *Observer*. His main stage plays include *Alphabetical Order*, *Donkeys' Years*, *Clouds*, *Make and Break*, *Noises Off*, *Benefactors*, *Wild Honey* (adapted from Chekhov's untitled play) and *Copenhagen*. He has done a number of translations, of Chekhov's plays in particular. His nine novels include *Towards the End of the Morning*, *The Trick of It*, *A Landing on the Sun* and *Headlong*, which was shortlisted for the Booker prize in 1999. Methuen has also published two selections of his columns, *The Original Michael Frayn* and *The Additional Michael Frayn*.

MICHAEL FRAYN

Plays: 3

Here
Now You Know
La Belle Vivette

introduced by the author

Methuen Drama

METHUEN CONTEMPORARY DRAMATISTS

3 5 7 9 10 8 6 4 2

This collection first published in the United Kingdom in 2000
by Methuen Publishing Limited
215 Vauxhall Bridge Road, London SW1V 1EJ

Here first published by Methuen Drama in 1993
Revised for this edition
Copyright © 1993, 2000 by Michael Frayn

Now You Know first published by Methuen Drama in 1995
Revised for this edition
Copyright © 1995, 2000 by Michael Frayn

La Belle Vivette first published in the programme for the ENO
production in 1995
Copyright © 1995, 2000 by Michael Frayn

Collection and introduction copyright © 2000 by Michael Frayn

The right of Michael Frayn to be identified as the author of these
works has been asserted by him in accordance with the Copyright,
Designs and Patents Act, 1988

Methuen Publishing Limited Reg. No. 3543167

A CIP catalogue record for this book
is available from the British Library

ISBN 0–413–75230–5

Typeset by Deltatype Ltd, Birkenhead, Merseyside
Printed and bound in Great Britain by
Cox & Wyman Ltd, Reading, Berkshire

Contents

Chronology   vi

Introduction   vii

HERE   1

NOW YOU KNOW   115

LA BELLE VIVETTE   231

A Chronology
of first performances

Jamie (television)   1968
Birthday (television)   1969
The Two of Us (Garrick)   1970
The Sandboy (Greenwich)   1971
Alphabetical Order (Hampstead; then Mayfair)   1975
Donkeys' Years (Globe)   1975
Clouds (Hampstead; then Duke of York's in 1978)   1975
Liberty Hall (Greenwich)   1979
Make and Break (Lyric, Hammersmith; then Theatre
    Royal, Haymarket)   1980
Noises Off (Lyric, Hammersmith; then Savoy)   1982
Benefactors (Vaudeville)   1984
Look Look (Aldwych)   1990
Here (Donmar)   1993
Now You Know (Hampstead)   1995
Copenhagen (Cottesloe, Royal National Theatre; then
    Duchess)   1998
Alarms & Excursions (Yvonne Arnaud, Guildford; then
    Gielgud)   1998

Translations and adaptions

The Cherry Orchard (from Chekhov: National Theatre) 1978
The Fruits of Enlightenment (from Tolstoy: National
    Theatre)   1979
Number One (from Anouilh: Queen's)   1984
Wild Honey (from Chekhov: National Theatre)   1984
Three Sisters (from Chekhov: Royal Exchange,
    Manchester)   1985
The Seagull (from Chekhov: Palace, Watford; then
    RSC, 1990)   1986
Uncle Vanya (from Chekhov: Vaudeville)   1988
The Sneeze (from Chekhov: Aldwych)   1988
Exchange (from Trifonov: Nuffield, Southampton; then
    Vaudeville)   1989
La Belle Vivette (from Offenbach: ENO, Coliseum)   1995

Introduction

Most of the plays in this volume were written and produced in the rather bleak part of my career that followed after the failure of *Look Look* in 1990 had put an abrupt end to the successes of the eighties, and before the kiss of life was most improbably administered eight years later by the success of *Copenhagen*. None of them failed as resoundingly as the wretched *Look Look* (only one good review; closed in less than a month) but they seemed to confirm the general rule that the longest a playwright can hope to remain on the upward slope is twenty years before the melancholy downward trudge back to his native obscurity begins.

Here did actually raise the total of good notices from one to four when it was produced at the Donmar in 1993, which I suppose was encouraging; but the other notices ranged from regretful disappointment, through mocking parody, to downright vituperation. You can sometimes learn a lot from bad reviews, as you probably can from any other form of punishment (though the lesson is usually a rather oblique one) and as I nursed my wounds I began to see that I had managed to put a lot of people's backs up in the very first scene, which had perhaps blinded them to what followed. People had leapt to the conclusion that it was to be an evening about the impossibility of human communication, the failure of feeling, and the meaninglessness of life; whereas it seemed to me about the way we do actually construct a world and a life for ourselves. I began to yearn to have another go at it. So when a production in New York was proposed and the director, Jason Buzas, suggested quite a lot of restructuring, I was very ready to listen. Buzas put forward a number of shrewd ideas that I have incorporated here, and I am very grateful to him.

The production in New York failed to materialise, but the revised version of the play has now been performed in a number of European countries. *Here* there has so far done a

lot better than *Here* here. This may suggest that the rewrites
have had some beneficial effect, or else that critical
standards are lower abroad; or perhaps merely that the title
needs a bit of work on it as well.

Since I have spent my life writing novels as well as plays,
one of the questions which people always ask is how I
decide whether a new idea is one for a play or for a novel.
The answer is that I don't. The matter decides itself. The
idea that takes shape inside one's head has its form written
upon it; that's what makes it an idea and not just a piece of
wishful thinking. The one exception to this simple rule is
Now You Know, which in its time has been both a novel and a
play.

It first presented itself to me as a play, and it was as a
play that I wrote it. I wrote many drafts of it, but they didn't
work, and I set it aside. Then it came to me that what the
story needed was to have access to the private thoughts of
each of the characters, and to their unspoken thoughts
about each other. So I wrote it as a novel, with the events
seen through the eyes of each of the eight characters in
turn. But, once the novel was published, I started thinking
about these people again. And now that I had been inside
each of their heads it seemed to me that it would be worth
making another attempt to tell the story as a play, where
one sees only as much of each person as he or she chooses
to reveal – or fails to keep concealed. Which is of course
how we are forced to see the people around us, all the time
we are not writing novels about them.

La Belle Vivette is my one venture into opera. Dennis Marks,
who was then Director of English National Opera, invited
me to translate Offenbach's *La Belle Hélène*, and I accepted
on condition that I could supply my own story and
characters, for reasons I have explained in the notes
attached to the text.

Writing lyrics turned out to be quite amazingly hard work – particularly since they had to be fitted to a pre-existing score. My guide and taskmaster was James Holmes, who was to conduct the piece, a man of legendary sweetness and boundless musicality. I was perpetually astonished by his ability to sit down at the piano with a new lyric, and accompany himself as he sang it at sight. I was perpetually cheered by the unfailing enthusiasm with which he did it; and chastened as he then gently explained that I had once again miscounted the beats in the bar and misplaced the natural stress, that I had once again piled inarticulable consonants upon unshapable vowels. I rewrote and rewrote and rewrote; it was almost as difficult as farce. When we had finished Jim sat down at a piano one Sunday afternoon in a rehearsal room at the Coliseum and played and sang all three acts through solo to Dennis, a feat so astonishing that it seemed to justify all my efforts in itself.

Rehearsals began, in the ENO's shabby warren of rehearsal rooms out near West Hampstead underground station. I went in almost every day, enchanted by the new world that I had wandered into. The dais at the front of the rehearsal room was divided into two separate kingdoms. The lefthand kingdom was ruled by Jim and the musical staff. The righthand realm belonged to the director, Ian Judge, and the production team. I don't know which half of the operation entranced me more. In all my years in the theatre I'd never seen such a director handle such a large cast or shape such an endlessly fluid piece of action in front of my eyes. I'd certainly never been involved in such a joyous flood of music-making. I had expected opera-singers to be difficult and temperamental; they turned out to be without exception charmingly good-natured and straightforward. I had expected them to save their voices during rehearsals by marking instead of singing out, but they all sang out almost all the time, from first thing in the morning until last thing at night.

In the event I don't think anyone heard many of the words I'd laboured so long over. The hugeness of the

Coliseum and its notorious acoustics swallowed them up, in spite of the efforts devoted by Jim and the cast to diction, and in spite of discreet miking. What words the critics did manage to catch they mostly didn't like. The original book, which had seemed so threadbare to me, was apparently to them a precious artistic heritage which had to be preserved from any attempt at restoration. We did nineteen performances, which is a respectable number in the opera house, and the audiences seemed to enjoy it; but then we did have the incomparable Lesley Garrett singing Vivette at most of the performances.

ENO were going to revive it in their 1999 season. But by then Dennis Marks had left, and Nicholas Payne, his successor, evidently abandoned the project. Or so I assume. No word was spoken, not at any rate to me, or to Jim, or to Ian Judge; but then large organisations, in my experience, rarely trouble to communicate with contributors for whom they have no further use. Eventually Tanya McCallin, who was designing *Manon* for them, told me that she had been given bits of our set to cannibalise. Well, it's one way of informing the next-of-kin.

So my one excursion into opera (or at least operetta) remains an isolated detour, a strenuous holiday from plays and novels. An intensely enjoyable one, though. And one day I like to think that perhaps someone might revive it – maybe in the way in which it was originally presented by Offenbach himself, not as a grand production in a major opera-house, but as a musical in a boulevard theatre, with a small chorus who can dance as well as sing and a small pit orchestra.

Michael Frayn
2000

Here

Here was first presented at the Donmar Warehouse Theatre, London, by arrangement with Michael Codron, on 29 July 1993, with the following cast:

Cath	Teresa Banham
Phil	Iain Glen
Pat	Brenda Bruce

Directed by Michael Blakemore
Designed by Ashley Martin-Davis
Lighting by Mark Henderson

Act One

An empty room.

Two doors. Window. Bare floor, bare walls, no furniture. A kitchenette cupboard, shelves, and an alcove with a curtain, now pulled back to reveal a rail with a few wire coat-hangers on it.

Scene One

One of the doors is unlocked and pushed open. On the threshold stands **Cath**, *holding the key on a label. She comes cautiously into the room, followed by* **Phil**. *They look dubiously around.*

Cath   No?

Phil   No. No?

Cath   No.

Phil *goes out.* **Cath** *takes a last look round. He reappears.*

Phil   What?

Cath   Nothing.

They both look round.

Not unless *you* . . . ?

Phil   Me? No.

He looks round again.

(*Reflectively.*) No. No. No. No . . . Why – what do *you* think?

Cath   No, no – if you think no.

Phil   You mean you *don't* think no?

Cath   No, I just think . . . I don't know . . .

Phil   You don't think *yes*? You're not saying you think *yes?*

Cath   No! No.

Phil   But you don't think no?

Cath   No, but since *you* think no.

Phil   I don't think no if *you* don't think no.

Cath   No, well . . .

They move about the room, looking. She opens the kitchenette.

Phil   What?

Cath   The cooker's a bit . . .

Phil   Yes.

She closes it. He opens the second door.

So's the bath.

She looks as well. He closes it. She pulls the curtain across to close off the alcove, then pulls it back again. She finds something in the corner of the alcove and picks it up.

Phil   What?

She holds it up – a worn toy dog.

Even the dog.

Cath   Yes – poor old dog.

He turns and looks out of the window.

What? The view?

She joins him at the window, still holding the dog. They look out.

Well . . .

Phil   Fine.

Cath   Reasonably.

Phil   Absolutely.

Cath Isn't it?

Phil Yes. Yes!

They move about the room again.

I just think it's all a bit ... I don't know ... A bit ...

Cath I suppose so.

She strokes the toy dog. Pause.

Phil I mean, we are both saying what we really think?
I can't bear it when we just say what we think each other
thinks.

Cath You mean when I do.

Phil When either of us does.

Cath Yes.

She absently cuddles the dog.

Phil Never mind that thing.

He takes it out of her hands and puts it down.

I'm just saying, if we don't know what each other actually
thinks ...

Cath I know.

Phil But you really do think ...?

Cath Yes! Yes!

Phil You mean, that it's a bit ...?

Cath A bit.

Phil Yes ...

Pause.

A bit what?

Cath What?

Phil I'm not absolutely clear what you mean.

Cath I mean . . . well . . .

Pause.

We could put the bed *here*.

Phil Oh. So you're saying . . . ?

Cath I'm not saying anything. I'm just saying we could put the bed here.

Phil I see.

Cath What?

Phil Nothing.

Cath Or there. That's all I'm saying. The bed could go there. Or here. In which case the table could go here.

Phil Yes. Well.

Cath What?

Phil I think we need to think about this.

Cath We *are* thinking about it.

Phil We *are* thinking about it?

Cath Aren't we?

Phil What – seriously *thinking* about it?

Cath Not *seriously* thinking about it. Just thinking about it . . .

Phil I see.

Cath You *said* – we ought to think about it!

Phil I mean go away and think about it.

Cath Go *away* and think about it?

Phil Cath, we were walking down the street! Five minutes ago! Just walking down the street, talking about . . . I don't know . . .

Cath The other place.

Phil What other place?

Cath The other place we're thinking about.

Phil I thought we *weren't* thinking about that one?

Cath I thought we were?

Phil Yes, well, anyway, never mind that . . .

Cath No, only that's what we were talking about . . .

Phil Right.

Cath I'm not trying to, you know . . .

Phil I know, I know. But the point is, we were walking down the street. We saw the board. We rang the bell . . . And that was five minutes ago! We didn't even know this place existed!

Cath No, but now we do.

Phil Now we do, yes, and all I'm saying is, it's something we can begin to think about.

Cath Yes . . .

Phil Cath, we're talking about something we're going to be looking at every single day of our lives. That's what we're deciding.

Cath I know.

Phil Not just one quick look – how does it seem? – fine – right, get the sandwiches out. We're not talking about a picnic-place.

Cath I know.

Phil We're talking about every day, day in, day out, for years and years to come. We're talking about lying here . . . yes?

Cath Or here.

Phil Or here, yes, and waking up every morning, and seeing . . . *this*. Right? These walls.

Cath Yes.

Phil This floor, this ceiling.

Cath Yes.

Phil *This*.

Cath I know.

Phil Every morning. Seven times a week. Thirty times a month. Three hundred and sixty-five times a year.

Cath We'd be away sometimes.

Phil And that's just for starters! We get up, we make breakfast, we sit here. What do we see?

Cath This.

Phil We have lunch, we have dinner. We read. We work. We talk to each other. And what do we see?

Cath We see this.

Phil Minute after minute. Hour after hour. We go to bed.

Cath Still this.

Phil Wake up next morning . . .

Cath We'd get used to it.

Phil Right. Exactly! We'd get used to it. That's what I'm saying. Is this what we want to get used to?

Cath But if it wasn't *this* room it would be somewhere else!

Phil Yes, but it *would* be this room! That's my point! Do you see?

Cath Well . . .

Phil   *These* walls. *This* floor. *This* ceiling. For ever.

Cath   Not for ever.

Phil   So for how long?

Cath   We don't know.

Phil   No. Indefinitely. No fixed term. At Her Majesty's pleasure. For ever.

Cath   Phil...

Phil   Look. One moment we're walking down the street, it's a nice day, anything could happen, we're thinking about this place, we're thinking about that place...

Cath   You said we *weren't* thinking about that place.

Phil   ... *not* thinking about that place – all right – then suddenly it's all decided!

Cath   But, Phil, *eventually*...

Phil   *Eventually*. Yes. *Eventually*.

Cath   We are *going* to...?

Phil   Decide? Yes. Of course. Of *course*. That's the point of thinking about things.

Pause.

Look. I'm getting at something important here, Cath. I don't know how to explain... Listen. Suppose we hadn't been walking down this street. Suppose we'd been walking down some other street. Yes? You can imagine that?

Cath   But we were in fact walking down this street.

Phil   Forget that. Yes?

Cath   But...

Phil   For the moment. All right? We'll come back to it. So, we're walking down another street. We see a board.

Some other board. Some other house. We ring the bell –
some other bell. So now we're not standing here. We're
standing in some totally different room. All right?

Cath   All right.

Phil   And what are we doing in this totally different
room?

Cath   We're having precisely the same conversation.

Phil   Exactly. We're contemplating a life looking at
completely different walls. Isn't that a bit strange? Doesn't
that seem slightly odd to you, Cath? I mean, I don't even
know *why* we were walking down this particular street!
We've never walked down it before. So why did we
today?

Cath   I don't know. We just did.

Phil   We just did. Yes. We just did.

Cath   But since we *did* . . .

Phil   Oh, sure. But isn't it a tiny bit . . . ?

Cath   What?

Phil   I don't know. A tiny bit . . . *indeterminate*?

Cath   Indeterminate?

Phil   I mean, look. We wouldn't have been walking
down this particular street or any other particular street if
. . . well . . . if we'd never met.

Cath   Never met? What are you talking about? What is
all this? We did meet, we did meet!

Phil   Yes, but we shouldn't have met if I hadn't gone to
that place where you were that day.

Cath   No . . .

Phil   And I shouldn't have gone to that place if I hadn't
known that man.

Cath All right.

Phil And I shouldn't have known that man if I hadn't walked up that mountain, and I shouldn't have walked up that mountain if there hadn't been a mountain to walk up, and there wouldn't have been a mountain to walk up if the rock strata hadn't been tilted the way they are, and the rock strata wouldn't have been tilted the way they are if the earth had cooled down differently five thousand million years ago, and if it had, Cath, if it had, if the earth had cooled down slightly differently five thousand million years ago, then I wouldn't be here now – *you* wouldn't be here now – you'd be standing in some completely different room with some completely different man.

Cath No, I shouldn't.

Phil Yes, you would. If you'd met someone else instead of me.

Cath If I'd met someone else instead of you?

Phil Yes.

Cath I shouldn't have fallen in love with them!

Phil Yes, you would. Of course you would. If I hadn't been there. You'd have fallen in love with *someone*.

Cath You mean, *you* would?

Phil All right.

Cath *You'd* be standing here with some completely different woman?

Phil Exactly! You see my point?

Pause.

Cath Yes.

She goes to the door.

Phil What?

Cath   Nothing.

Phil   Where are you going?

Cath   Away. To think about it. You said.

Phil   Hold on.

Cath   What?

Phil   What's going on?

Cath   What do you mean, what's going on?

Phil   Why are you being like this all of a sudden?

Cath   Like what?

Phil   Like this.

Cath   Come on.

She opens the door.

Phil   Just a moment.

He closes the door.

Cath   Do you mind?

She opens the door.

Phil   I do mind.

He closes the door.

Cath   I want to go.

She opens the door.

Phil   I don't want to go.

He closes the door.

Not until you tell me.

Cath   Tell you what?

Phil   What this is all about.

Cath   You know what this is all about.

Phil   I don't know what this is all about.

Cath   Well, you do, as a matter of fact.

Phil   Well, I don't, as a matter of fact.

Cath   Year after year. That's what you said. Day in, day out. Stuck here for ever. No fixed term.

Phil   I don't mean *us*!

Cath   You might find something better. You might be here with some totally different woman.

Phil   That's what you're worrying about?

Cath   *I'm* not worrying about it. *You're* worrying about it.

Phil   Not about *us*, Cath! I'm not worrying about *us*!

Cath   That's what you're saying.

Phil   No.

Cath   Walls, floors – us.

Phil   Not us.

Cath   Let's go.

Phil   Listen. Love. We're the one bit that's decided!

Cath   Are we?

Phil   Aren't we?

Cath   I don't know.

Phil   You don't know? You do know! You do! You know!

Cath   Yes. Well. Let's think about it.

Phil   Let's think about it?

Cath   We're thinking about everything else.

Phil   Exactly. Everything else. That's why we're

thinking about it. Because it's everything else. We don't have to think about us. We've thought about us.

Cath   *I've* thought about us.

Phil   *You've* thought about us. *I've* thought about us. *We've* thought about us. We're us. That's fixed. That's the problem. It's how we think about everything else. How *we* think about everything else. How we think as *us*. How we shape our world. How we decide.

Cath   How we decide?

Phil   That's what this is all about. Isn't it?

Cath   You mean how *you* decide.

Phil   No. How *we* decide. How you and I decide.

Cath   Oh. Well, don't worry about me. I've decided.

Phil   You've *decided?* *You've* decided? Cath!

Cath   One of us has to decide. One of us has to decide *something!* And if *you're* not going to decide then *I'm* going to decide, and I've decided.

Phil   Decided what?

Cath   Decided no. So, off we go.

Phil   Hold on.

Cath   Look, don't mess around. I've got things to do.

Phil   Yes, but *I've* decided, too.

Cath   Well, then, that's all right.

Phil   I've decided yes.

Cath   You've decided yes?

Phil   Yes.

Cath   No, you haven't.

Phil   Yes, I have.

Cath You don't like it.

Phil Not much.

Cath But you've decided yes?

Phil Yes.

Cath Oh.

Phil Peculiar, isn't it.

Cath Most peculiar.

Phil Almost as peculiar as liking it and deciding no.

Cath I don't like it.

Phil Yes, you do.

Cath I don't.

Phil You do.

Cath Don't tell me what I like!

Phil You like it.

Cath I hate it! As a matter of fact. So. *I* hate it. *You* hate it. *We* hate it.

Phil I rather like it.

Cath You said you *didn't* like it.

Phil When did I say I didn't like it?

Cath About half-a-minute ago!

Phil *You* said I didn't like it.

Cath And you agreed!

Phil I was wrong.

Cath What do you mean, you were wrong? How could you be wrong?

Phil Very easily. It's very easy to be wrong.

Cath   Not about whether you *like* something! You must know whether you *like* something or not!

Phil   No. It's often extremely difficult.

Pause.

Cath   You mean me.

Phil   What?

Cath   You mean you don't like me.

Phil   Don't like you?

Cath   Is that what you're saying?

Phil   Just a moment. I say, I like this place. You say, You mean you don't like me . . . ?

Cath   You said you *didn't* like it . . .

Phil   *You* said I didn't like it!

Cath   You said you didn't know whether you liked it or not.

Phil   No, I didn't. What I said was . . . I don't know . . . I can't remember what I said. I don't know what we're talking about.

Cath   *I* don't know what we're talking about. I don't know what's happening to us. I just want to get out of here.

Pause.

Please.

Pause.

Can we go? Please? Phil?

Phil   Yes. I'm sorry. I just felt . . . I don't know . . .

Cath   Yes. Well. It doesn't matter.

Phil   I just felt all kind of . . . walls and ceilings. You know?

Cath   Honestly, Phil. Sometimes . . .

Phil   Pressing in.

Cath   I'm not trying to trap you!

Phil   I know, I know.

Cath   I'm not trying to talk you into anything!

Phil   It's seeing that other place. Then this place . . .

Cath   You're absolutely free to do whatever you want!

Phil   It'll be better when we've found somewhere. When we've got everything settled.

He opens the door.

Cath   Will it?

Phil   Won't it?

Cath   Perhaps it will.

Phil   I think it will, Cath.

Cath   Yes . . .

She moves to go out. He stops her.

Phil   I'm sorry, Cath. I'm sorry! My fault. All my fault. As usual.

Cath   Well, I expect *I* was . . .

Phil   No, you weren't!

Cath   I was, as a matter of fact.

Phil   You weren't, as a matter of fact.

Cath   Well . . .

Phil   No. As a matter of fact. As it happens.

Cath   Anyway.

Phil   Anyway.

He holds the door open for her. She hesitates.

Cath   Phil . . .

Phil   What?

Cath   You do . . . ?

Phil   Do what?

Cath   Like me?

Phil   Yes.

Cath   A bit?

Phil   Yes.

Pause.

Yes! As a matter of fact. As it happens.

Cath   Just a bit?

He closes the door.

Phil   I love you.

Cath   Do you?

Phil   You know I do.

Cath   Perhaps.

Phil   I do.

Cath   Yes.

Phil   I do.

He kisses her.

Yes?

Cath   Yes.

He opens the door.

Phil . . .

Phil What?

She closes the door.

What?

Cath *I* love *you.*

Phil Yes.

Cath How do you mean, yes?

Phil I mean I know.

Cath You don't know, as a matter of fact.

Phil I do know, as a matter of fact.

Cath Sometimes.

Phil Always.

Cath Not always.

Phil Now, though.

Cath Maybe.

They kiss.

Phil So . . . Yes?

Cath Yes?

Phil This place.

Cath Oh . . . !

She laughs.

Phil What?

Cath You.

Phil Why?

Cath Funny.

Phil Why funny?

Cath Sweet.

They kiss.

Phil   Funny if I'm sweet?

Cath   Very funny.

Phil   I'm always sweet.

Cath   No, you're not.

Phil   Yes, I am.

Cath   You're always arguing.

Phil   No, I'm not.

Cath   Yes, you are.

Phil   I'm not arguing now.

Cath   You *are* arguing now.

Phil   Me?

Cath   You.

Phil   *I* say I'm not arguing. *You* say I'm arguing . . .

Cath   You're saying *I'm* arguing?

Phil   All I'm saying is . . . yes.

He kisses her.

Yes. OK? Yes. Yes. Yes?

Cath   No.

Phil   No?

Cath   Isn't that what you want me to say?

Phil   What *I* want you to say?

Cath   Isn't it?

Phil   I'm saying yes!

Cath   Yes, you're being very sweet.

Phil   So?

Cath   So *I'm* being very sweet back.

Phil   And saying no?

Cath   Then you can be very sweet back to me and say all right, no.

Phil   Cath! Love! We're going round in circles! I'm not saying no. I'm saying yes. Quite straightforwardly – yes. All right?

Pause.

Cath   All right.

Phil   You're agreeing?

Cath   Yes.

Phil   So it's yes?

Cath   Yes!

Pause.

Phil   Only you're not agreeing.

Cath   I am!

Phil   You're not! I can see by the look on your face.

She laughs.

What?

Cath   Nothing.

She puts her hands over her face, and laughs.

Phil   Why are you laughing?

Cath   I'm not laughing.

She laughs. He waits. She stops laughing.

I'm not. In fact.

Phil   All right . . .

Cath   All right what?

Phil   All right, *no*.

Pause.

Cath   All right.

Phil   That's what you're saying, isn't it? I say yes. You don't agree. You're saying no.

Cath   I'm saying no.

*Enter **Pat**, a woman in her sixties. She looks at each of them.*

Pat   Or do you want to think about it?

Phil   No, no. (*To **Cath**.*) Well . . .

Cath   No.

Pat   The roof's been done. I had the roof done. You won't have any trouble with the roof.

Phil   I think we think . . . (*To **Cath**.*) Don't we?

Cath   We think it's very nice.

Phil   Very nice! (*To **Cath**.*) Only I thought you thought . . . ?

Cath   I thought it was very nice.

Pause.

Pat   This was the boys' room.

Cath   Oh.

Pat   Peter's bed was there. David's bed was there. Lucy was downstairs opposite me.

Cath   Yes, I'm sorry. You must feel a bit . . .

Pat   What?

Cath   Having strangers in here.

Pat   What, go through all that again? No, thank you! Up and down the stairs. Bad dreams, drinks of water. 'Now if you two don't tidy this room I don't know what I shall do!' Slaps, fights. Hugs, kisses. 'This room – it's a disgrace!' Crash crash crash on the ceiling – what are they up to up there? Then nothing – silence – they're out all night – where are they? You two come wandering in, stars in your eyes, you think an empty room, that's all you need – you don't know what you're starting.

Phil Yes . . .

Cath Well . . .

Pat Now what? David's up north, Peter's all over the place, he's very big in Europe, Lucy's living with some woman in a caravan – 'Mum, I'm a lesbian.' Meanwhile I've got their old vaccination records downstairs, I've got microscopes, I've got electrical this, I've got electrical that, I've got a whole cat-basket full of doll's clothes, I can't move down there. While here you are, empty room, you think it's not going to happen to you.

Pause.

Phil Anyway . . .

Pat Then we put Mum in here. Bed there, her piano there, her old walnut dining-room suite. All her knick-knacks. It was like a furniture shop. You couldn't move! I said, 'Mum, this is worse than the boys!' She said, 'You won't have to put up with it for very long, Pat.' Oh, won't I? I put up with it for seven years. Bang bang on the ceiling. Up and down the stairs. 'Never mind, Pat, you won't have to put up with it for much longer now.' She died in my arms! Gave me a smile and died in my arms!

She weeps.

Cath I'm sorry . . .

Pat *recovers herself.*

Pat *I'm* not. I'm glad. Glad you can get it all behind you. Settle down. Be on your own. Not have to think about other people all day long. You? You've got it all to come. You think I envy you? I don't. I don't.

Pause.

Phil We must . . .

He moves towards the door.

Pat I made up a bed in here for Eric. This was the year after I lost Mum. He'd come up here nights when his cough was bad and then he could cough away on his own. Cough cough. Cough cough. All night, no rest from it. Cough cough. Cough cough. He thought I couldn't hear him up here. I could hear him. Cough cough. But of course I never said, so he thought I was asleep, it was easier for *him*. Poor lamb. Coughed his heart out. He coughed *my* heart out. Him awake up here, me awake down there. Poor old love.

Cath When did he . . . ?

Pat Four years ago. They took his lung out, but it was all over him by then, he was riddled with it. Seven weeks in the hospital, nine weeks in the nursing home, and that was it. That was the end of the story. So it's all behind me. And if you think I'd want to be you, empty room, honey this, lovey that, and everything still to come, then you're much mistaken.

Cath Yes . . .

Phil Cath . . .

He holds the door open.

Pat I shouldn't have told you all that. You want to come into an empty room. Fresh paint, a few bits and pieces of your own, blank page, chapter one, nothing ever happened in the world before.

Phil So we'll ring the agent . . .

He goes out. **Pat** *waits at the door.* **Cath** *takes one last look* *round. She picks up the toy dog.*

Pat (*to* **Cath**)   That was the last couple. You always leave something behind when you go, don't you. There's always one thing.

Cath   They had a child? In here?

Pat   Oh, she was lovely! Little fingers, little smile. I could have eaten her!

Phil *reappears.*

Phil   What?

Cath   Nothing.

She puts the toy dog down. Pause. She goes to the door.

(*To* **Pat**.) But if we didn't do it through the agent? If we split the commission . . . ?

Phil (*alarmed*)   What do you mean?

Cath   Nothing. I was just wondering . . .

They all go out.

Blackout.

Scene Two

A mattress now occupies the centre of the room, with a small TV and an alarm clock on the floor beside it. A simple table, with two chairs. By the window stands a small pot-plant. On the wall, a picture or two. There are a few objects carefully arranged on the shelves, including the toy dog. The curtain is drawn across the alcove.

Phil *and* **Cath** *are sitting on the mattress, looking at the room. They are wearing identical jumpers. He has his arms round her.*

Phil   Yes?

Cath   Yes. Yes!

Phil   Yes . . .

Pause.

Or . . .

He gets up and goes towards the shelves.

Cath   Come back!

Phil   What?

Cath   Don't go away!

Phil   Just . . .

Cath   What?

Phil   This.

He moves the toy dog to a new position.

Better?

Cath   Better.

Phil   Or worse?

Cath   Better. Isn't it?

Phil   Yes. Much better.

He returns to the mattress, and puts his arms round her.

Yes?

Cath   Yes!

He looks round the room.

Phil   Cath, I think . . . I *think* . . .

Cath   . . . we've got it.

Phil   I *think*.

Cath   I think we have.

Phil   I think we may just possibly have.

Cath   *You* have.

Phil   *We* have.

Cath   *You* did it.

Phil   *We* did it.

Cath   Anyway, we're there.

Phil   So . . .

Cath   So we can just . . . I don't know!

Phil   Sit back.

Cath   Yes! Sit back and . . . what?

Phil   Live. Or whatever.

Cath   Oh, love . . .

She kisses him. He looks at the shelves.

Phil   Hold on.

Cath   What?

He jumps up and goes back to the shelves.

What are you doing?

Phil   Nothing.

He moves the toy dog to the floor by the bed, and the alarm clock to the shelf where the dog was.

Cath   You're moving him?

Phil   No. I just wanted to see if the clock . . .

Cath   Leave it, leave it!

She holds out her arms to him.

Phil   Just a moment . . .

He moves it again.

Cath   You had it right before!

Phil   Yes, but I just wanted to try something . . .

He moves it again.

How about that?

Cath Fine.

Phil Yes?

Cath Yes!

Phil So that's what we're deciding?

Cath That's what we're deciding.

He gazes at it.

Phil Now?

Cath What?

Phil We're actually now in the process of deciding it?

Cath Yes! Yes!

Pause.

Phil I somehow can't . . . *feel* myself deciding it.

Cath *I've* decided.

Phil You've decided?

Cath Yes.

Phil You *have* decided? You've *finished* deciding?

Cath Ages ago. Come on!

Phil How do you know you've finished deciding?

Cath Phil!

Phil No, I'm making a serious point. How do we *know* when we're deciding something?

Cath All right – put him back where he was, then.

Phil Put him back?

Cath If you want to.

Phil   If we put him back *here*, then we *didn't* decide to put him *there*.

Cath   *You* didn't.

Phil   *You* didn't! You thought you did, but you didn't.

Cath   Well, I did!

Phil   You can't have done, since the result was that he ended up *here*! Now, let's try again. And this time let's make absolutely sure we are conscious of the decision being made.

Cath   Oh, put him anywhere.

Phil   What do you mean?

Cath   It doesn't really matter, does it?

Phil   Doesn't *matter*?

Cath   It's not going to start a world war if you put the dog there instead of there!

Phil   It might! We don't know!

Cath   Don't be silly, love.

Phil   Cath, we can't foresee what the consequences will be! We're standing at a crossroads . . .

Cath   What – putting it there or putting it there?

Phil   Putting it there or putting it there – and there's no signpost, and we can't possibly see where the two different paths lead. All we know is that whichever one we take, that's the one we'll have taken.

Cath   We can always move it.

Phil   That won't alter the fact that it was here to start with. It will always *have been* here. We'll have that with us for ever. For ever and ever. It's like looking up at the sky at night. We're staring into infinity.

Cath   Yes, well, I don't want to think about it.

Phil   All right, then we won't think about it.

Cath   Do you mind?

Phil   Then on and on the effects of not thinking about it will go . . .

Cath   Yes, but let's not even talk about it.

Phil   And if we don't even talk about it . . .

Cath   I know.

Phil   If we don't talk about not even talking about it . . .

Cath   I know. I *know*!

Phil   But, Cath . . .

Cath   Don't. Don't. Sorry. But just . . . don't.

Pause.

Phil   Cath, all I'm saying is – we've got to take control.

Cath   Yes.

Phil   Because here we are.

Cath   Here we are.

Phil   Now.

Cath   Yes.

Phil   As it happens.

Cath   How do you mean, as it happens?

Phil   I mean, if we hadn't seen the board that day . . .

Cath   Oh no! Don't start all that again!

Phil   No, but if we *hadn't* . . .

Cath   You'd have gone off with some other woman – I know, I know!

Phil   That's not what I said . . .

She gets up from the bed, goes to the table, and opens books to work.

Cath Just put it all where you want it.

Pause. He looks at her.

Go on! Put it wherever you want it!

Phil Put it wherever *I* want it? Cath!

Cath I don't know what you mean, it all just *happened*.

Phil I mean things happened that we didn't decide . . .

Cath But we *did* decide!

Phil In the end.

Cath We decided about *this* place!

Phil Exactly. We took over . . .

Cath We walked down the street, we saw the board, we looked at this place, and we *decided*!

Phil Yes, so now we've got to go *on* deciding.

Cath 'It all just happened'! It *didn't* all just happen! We made it happen!

Phil That's what I'm saying! We're saying the same thing!

Cath This is us.

Phil Yes! That's why it's so important that we know when we're deciding and when we're not. Because now we've started we have to go on deciding together. On and on.

Cath Till death us do part.

Pause.

Phil Cath, what *is* all this?

Cath What is all what?

Phil All this great thing?

Cath All what great thing? I don't know what you're talking about.

Pause.

Phil All right, I'll put it back.

He drags the mattress to the side of the room.

Cath What's happening?

Phil That's what this is all about.

Cath The bed?

Phil Isn't it?

Cath No, I agreed!

Phil Did you?

Cath I said! If you want to put in the middle of the room, then put it in the middle of the room! I agreed!

Pause.

Phil You agreed, yes, but you didn't mean it. Your agreement was *inauthentic*.

Cath Inauthentic?

Phil Inauthentic.

Pause. Then she drags the mattress back to the middle of the room.

No, no, no, no, no, no, no.

He drags it back to the periphery.

If you want it here . . . then I agree.

Cath You don't!

Phil I've just said I do!

Cath You say you do but you don't! Your agreement is . . . what was the word?

Phil   Inauthentic? Is that what you're saying? My agreement is *inauthentic*?

She sits down and resumes her work. Pause.

Look. Look. I wanted it there. Yes. That's true. I was making a very simple point. The things around us, it seems to me, should give natural expression to the form of our life. Now, what is the centre of our life? The centre of our life is our being together. Yes? Our being one. Yes? What is the physical embodiment of our being one? Our making love. Where do we make love?

Cath   On this chair, sometimes.

Phil   Sometimes.

Cath   On that chair.

Phil   Never mind the chairs. We make love on this bed. If making love is at the centre of our life, then this bed ought to be in the centre of the room. That's all I'm saying. I simply felt that having the bed in the centre was more . . .

Cath   Authentic.

Pause.

Phil   You don't *really* want it here, do you?

She goes back to work.

Do you?

No response.

All right, then let me ask you one simple question. How do you *know* you want it here?

Cath   How do I *know* I want it there?

Phil   How, in actual fact, do you *know* you want it here?

Cath   I just do.

Phil   Oh. You just do.

Cath   All right?

Phil   All right. Fine. Wonderful. You just know you want it here. Well, I just know you *don't* want it here.

Cath   You just know I don't want it there?

Phil   Yes.

Cath   So how do you just know that?

Phil   I just do. The same as you just do.

Cath   But I'm me and you're you!

Phil   Also because I know you're simply trying to make a point. Because no one in the entire world could possibly want the bed here.

Cath   Except me.

Pause.

Phil   (*pleads*)   Cath! We had things almost right!

Cath   We don't have to have things right. We can have them wrong if we want to.

Phil   Yes, but we don't *want* them wrong!

Cath   *I* want them wrong!

She jumps up and starts to rearrange things at random.

I want the dog here! I want the clock here!

She sits down again. Pause. **Phil** *keeps very calm.*

Phil   I think what you feel – and I accept the authenticity of your feeling – is that there is some natural order in the universe according to which the table and chairs should be more central than the bed.

Cath   I just think there's something a bit funny about having the bed in the middle of the room.

Phil   A bit funny?

Cath But if we're talking about the natural order of things in the universe . . .

Cath *gets up and drags the mattress back to the centre of the room.*

. . . then the natural order of things in the universe is where you want them, so we might as well just put them there and have done with it.

Phil No!

He drags it back to the periphery.

If you don't accept my arguments then agreeing to put it there is completely . . .

Cath Where did you pick up this ridiculous word?

Phil What word?

Cath Inauthentic.

Phil I didn't say inauthentic.

Cath No, you were just about to.

Phil I wasn't, as a matter of fact.

Cath Oh, what were you going to say?

Phil I'm not going to tell you.

Pause. She laughs.

Cath Phil, honestly!

Pause. He laughs.

Honestly!

Pause. They have stopped laughing.

Phil Also, you're wearing my jumper again.

Cath This? This is *my* jumper.

He smells the arm of the jumper he is wearing.

Phil *This* is your jumper.

She sniffs the arm of the jumper she is wearing.

Cath   It's not!

Phil   It is, as a matter of fact.

Cath   Anyway, since they're exactly the same . . .

Phil   They're not exactly the same!

Cath   What's the difference?

Phil   What's the difference? One's yours and one's mine. That's the difference.

Pause. He looks at the mattress.

I mean, we've got to have some way of deciding things. That's all I'm saying. If people are trying to decide things they've got to have some method, some constitutional procedure, some agreed principles they can refer to.

Cath   Not necessarily.

Phil   So how *do* we decide things, then?

Cath   The same way as everybody else. We fight.

Phil   Fight?

Cath   Why not?

Phil   How?

Cath   Like this.

She grabs his ankle and tips him backwards on to the mattress.

I've won!

Phil   That's not fair!

Cath   So the bed stays here.

Phil   But I wasn't ready!

He jumps up.

All right. If you want to fight, we'll fight.

They stand on the mattress, facing each other.

All right?

Cath All right.

Phil You say, then.

Cath What do you want me to say?

Phil Say ready steady.

Cath Ready steady?

Phil Yes . . .

Cath Go!

She grabs his ankle, and tips him over backwards.

Phil Don't be ridiculous!

Cath What?

He gets up.

Phil You can't just say go!

Cath I said ready steady!

Phil You said ready steady query.

Cath I didn't say ready steady query.

Phil You did!

Cath I said ready steady go!

She grabs his ankle, and tips him over backwards.

Phil Cath, that's *cheating!*

He attempts to get up. She squats on top of him.

Get off! You've still got to have *rules,* even if you're
fighting! Cath, will you get off me . . . ? You can't just
knock people down and jump on them! Also you're
crushing my balls. Pax! Cath, I said pax . . .

She pulls the duvet up around them.

Cath We've fallen into a snowdrift! We're at the South Pole!

Phil Cath, stop messing around . . .

Cath The wind's howling. It's dark. We don't know where we are.

She lies full length on top of him, in the confusion of the duvet.

Phil What's all this?

Cath We'll freeze to death. We'll die. The wind's blowing us away . . .

They begin to roll away off the mattress, wrapped in the duvet. There is a knocking at the door.

We're out of control!

Phil What's that banging?

Cath Stop us, someone! We're going to roll off the edge of the world . . . !

Phil Hold on . . .

Cath Help! Help!

More knocking at the door.

Phil Cath . . .

Pat (*off*) Cath?

They stop rolling.

Are you all right?

They sit up.

Cath!

Phil *begins to get to his feet.* **Cath** *restrains him.*

Cath (*whispers*) She'll go away . . .

They wait.

Pat (*off*)   Cath, it's me.

More urgent knocking.

Phil (*to* **Pat**)   Coming!

He goes to open the door.

Cath (*whispers*)   Wait!

Phil   What?

She indicates the state of the room.

Phil   We can't start . . .

Pat (*off*)   Phil?

Phil (*to* **Pat**)   Yes, coming!

Cath   Bed! Bed!

She straightens out the bedclothes.

Pat (*off*)   What's going on in there?

Phil (*calls*)   Just coming! (*Whispers.*) All right?

Cath   Yes!

He goes to open the door.

No!

Phil   What?

Cath   Chair!

She pulls the curtain back on the alcove, and reveals a world of hanging clothes, cardboard boxes, cleaning materials, and odd random possessions. From the midst of the confusion **Cath** *drags out an upright easy chair. Avalanches of junk come tumbling into the room around it.*

Phil   Never mind about that!

Cath   Yes! Help me!

He helps her get the chair free of the confusion, and place it in the middle of the room.

Phil   We can't do this every time she comes!

The door is shaken in its frame.

Pat (*off*)   Phil? What's happening?

Phil   Coming! Coming! (*Whispers.*) This is mad!

Cath   Open the door, then!

Phil *opens the door.*

Phil   Come in.

Pat (*very alarmed*)   Where's Cath?

Cath   Come in!

Pat   Oh, there you are. As long as you're all right . . . I won't come in.

She comes in.

I'm not coming in.

Cath   Sit down.

Phil   Sit down.

They indicate the chair they have placed. **Pat** *remains standing.*

Pat   I don't want to keep running up the stairs.

Cath   No, please.

Pat   Dropping in all the time.

Cath   Sit down!

She remains standing.

Pat   Only – crash on the ceiling.

Phil   Oh, sorry, yes, that was me. I fell over.

Pat   Then crash again.

Phil   Yes, I got up, and . . .

Cath We were talking about where things should go.

Pat Then crash a third time.

Phil We were messing around.

Pat I thought – oh no, here we go again. Last couple up here – just like you – not a stick of furniture – nothing – all over each other. Honey this, lovey that. All very nice, only then of course the shouting started, then the screaming started. 'You swore on your mother's grave!' That's her. Scream scream. That's *him*! Screaming his lungs out! I've never heard anything like it! This door? I thought they'd have it off the hinges. Slam! She goes running down the stairs. Meanwhile everything up here's going smash. Smash smash smash. All the glasses, all the plates. Then they had the *baby*.

Pause.

So I hear crash on the ceiling tonight I think, here we go again.

Cath Yes. Thank you.

Pat I can still feel my heart pounding.

Phil Sit down.

He indicates the chair. **Pat** *looks at it but remains standing.*

Pat You think Poor old soul, comes running up here at the slightest squeak, she feels sorry for herself. I'll tell you who the poor old soul feels sorry for – she feels sorry for you.

Cath Yes.

Phil Anyway . . .

He indicates the chair again. **Pat** *has begun to calm down.*

Pat Still here, then, is it? I thought it'd be behind that curtain by now.

Phil No . . .

Cath   No!

Pat *looks at the tumbled confusion from behind the curtain.*

Pat   What, runs out every time it hears me coming?

Cath   Of course not.

Phil   Sits here waiting for you. Pining away. Its little paws in the air.

Pat   I thought you might be glad of it.

Cath   We are.

Pat   If you don't want it, put it out for the dustman.

Cath   Of course we want it.

Pat   That was Eric's chair.

Cath   I know.

Pat   He always sat in that chair.

Pause.

Cath (*to* **Pat**)   Tea? Coffee? Anything?

Pat   I'm not staying.

Pat *sits down on one of the other chairs.* **Phil** *offers Eric's chair to* **Cath**.

Pat   Anybody else sat there he wouldn't say anything.

Cath *sits down on the other original chair.* **Phil** *sits down in Eric's chair.*

Phil   But you'd know.

Pat   'What's the matter?' I'd go to him.

Phil   'Nothing,' he'd go.

Cath *looks at him.*

Phil   What?

She looks away.

Pat 'Oh, your chair.' 'It doesn't matter.'

Phil You'd have to tell them.

Pat I'd have to tell them. 'You're sitting in Eric's chair!'

Phil Then afterwards . . .

Pat Afterwards, oh! 'You shouldn't have said that!' 'Said what?' 'Said it was my chair!'

Phil Always your fault, isn't it.

Cath *looks at him.*

Phil What?

Cath Nothing.

Pat What?

Phil Nothing.

Pause. **Pat** *is gradually relaxing.*

Pat Oh, that's much better, Cath. Your mattress. Up in the corner there.

Cath Oh. Yes.

Phil You like it?

Pat Looked a bit funny out here in the middle of the room.

Phil A bit funny?

Pat I never liked to say.

Phil (*to* **Cath**) A bit funny. You see?

Pat Oh, now I've done it.

Phil No, you tell her, Pat. She won't listen to me.

Pat Only the last lot were like that. Bedclothes everywhere. You didn't know where to look. Then of course it all started. Crash. Bang. I came running up here. Nothing but broken glass and blood all over his face. And the cot standing in the middle of it all. Poor little mite.

Cath   Phil doesn't want it up there.

Pat   Oh, he's the one?

Phil   *I* don't want it up there? I *put* it up there!

Cath   He thinks it's inauthentic.

Pat   Oh, I see. It's what?

Cath   Inauthentic.

Phil   Inauthentic? Is that what I think?

Cath   It's his new word.

Phil (*to* **Pat**)   I say these strange things.

Cath   The last one was 'over-determinate'.

Phil (*to* **Pat**)   'Over-determinate'! Can you imagine?

Cath   Over-determinate is what it would be if we had more than two chairs.

Phil   More than three chairs, I think you mean, my love.

Cath   More than three chairs.

Phil (*to* **Pat**)   We agree about some things.

Cath   Also *indeterminate*.

Phil   We don't agree about indeterminate.

Cath   Indeterminate is what it is if the bathroom door isn't closed.

Phil (*to* **Cath**)   Not at all. It doesn't have to be closed.

Cath   What do you mean? It has to be closed!

Phil   No, it can be open.

Cath   It can't be open!

Phil   It can be *fully* open.

He opens it to demonstrate.

Cath   Oh, *fully* open . . .

Phil   But not half-open.

He demonstrates.

Cath (*to* **Pat**)   Not half-open.

Phil (*to* **Pat**)   Yes, because she's always half-doing things! If she puts a book down it's half on the table and half off the table. If she's doing the washing-up she half does it and half doesn't. If she starts saying something she says half of it and then . . .

He stops.

Cath   Then what?

Phil   Exactly!

Cath   Anyway, don't drag Pat into all this nonsense!

Phil   Don't drag Pat into it? You're telling *me* not to drag Pat into it? Pat – did *I* drag you into this?

Pat   I'm not saying a word, my loves. Leave me right out of it.

Cath   I know what Pat thinks.

Phil   Oh, you know what Pat thinks?

Pat   None of us says anything we can't say anything wrong.

Cath   Yes.

Phil   Yes!

Pat   So, thank you, Cath, thank you, Phil . . .

She gets to her feet.

Phil   Where are you going?

Cath   Sit down!

Pat *sits, reluctantly.*

Pat   Only I don't want to start anything.

Cath   You're not.

Phil   You're stopping it.

Pat   Yes. Well.

Pause.

That plant's coming on, Cath.

Cath   Yes.

Phil   Yes!

Cath   What?

Phil   Nothing.

Pat   It likes being by the window there.

Phil   It does indeed.

Pause.

Pat   Have I said something?

Cath   No.

Phil   No, no. No, no.

Cath (*to* **Phil**)   What?

Phil   Nothing.

Pause.

Pat   Eric was a great one for pot-plants. 'You know what you are?' I used to say to him. 'You're pot-potty.'

Pause.

Cath (*to* **Phil**)   I don't know what you're talking about!

Phil (*to* **Pat**)   *It* likes it there. *She* wants it *here*.

Cath I *don't* want it here!

Phil Oh. I thought you did?

Cath *You* want it here!

Phil *I* want it here?

Cath You said 'It has to go here'!

Phil Yes. If the bed goes *there*.

Cath Pat . . .

Phil Never mind Pat. Pat can see for herself. If the bed goes *there* then there's a space *here* . . .

He gets up to demonstrate.

. . . so that if you want the bed *there* then you want the plant *here*. Logically.

Cath Oh, don't start saying 'logically'!

Phil No, but it's half-doing things again.

Cath Phil, I shall murder you.

Phil No, you won't. You'll half-murder me.

Pat Listen, my loves . . .

Cath Yes, tell him, will you, Pat?

Phil All right, let's ask Pat.

Pat You *can't* put the plant there, because there's no light.

Cath That's precisely what I'm saying.

Phil That's precisely the point I'm making.

Pat So put the *chair* there.

She moves Eric's chair into the empty space.

Phil The chair? We don't want the chair there!

He moves it back to its original position.

Cath   You want the chair *here*?

Phil   I want the chair here.

Cath   No, you don't!

She moves it into the space.

Phil   Yes, I do!

He moves it back to its original position.

Cath   You *don't*!

She moves it into the space.

Phil   I *do*!

He moves it back to its original position.

Cath   You don't want it anywhere! You want it behind there!

Phil   No, I don't. Of course I don't. (*To* **Pat**.) I don't!

Pause.

Pat   You don't want that chair?

Phil   Of course we want this chair!

He looks at **Cath**.

Cath   Of course we do.

Phil   We like it. We both do.

Pat   That was Eric's chair.

Phil   We know.

Cath   He likes it really. He does.

Pause.

Pat   I'll give it to the jumble.

She picks up the chair and takes it to the door with her.

Phil   Pat, don't be silly!

Pat You don't want me coming up you've only got to say.

She goes out, carrying the chair. Pause.

Cath Sorry.

Phil (*gently*) We *agreed*.

Cath Yes.

Phil Behind the thing. *I* agreed – *you* agreed.

Cath Sorry.

Phil Anyway, we've got rid of it.

They look at each other and laugh. Then she stops laughing.

Cath I'd better go down.

She hesitates.

Hadn't I?

Phil She'll give you it back.

Cath It was Eric's chair!

Phil Eric hated it!

Cath What do you mean?

Phil She said – he used to come up here.

Cath That was later. That was when he was ill.

Phil Cough cough.

Cath I'd better go down . . .

Phil Coughed all over little Arthur and Cyril.

Cath That was before.

Phil Arthur was here. Cyril was there.

Cath Don't.

Phil Don't what?

Cath   It's sad.

Phil   Heartbreaking . . .

He coughs.

Cath   Phil!

Phil   She can't hear.

Cath   I don't care.

He coughs more loudly.

Anyway, she might. She heard *him*.

Phil   That was . . .

He coughs heartbreakingly.

Cath   Sh! She might still be there . . .

She nods at the door.

Phil   Where?

She nods at the door again.

Outside the door?

Cath   Don't shout.

Phil   She isn't.

Cath   She could be.

Phil   She wouldn't.

Cath   Why not? It's her landing.

Phil   It's our door.

Cath   It's her house.

*Pause. Then **Phil** goes to the door.*

Cath   What?

Phil   Open it.

Cath   Don't!

Phil   See if she's there.

Cath   No!

Phil   Why not?

Cath   Because supposing she was.

Phil   What do you mean?

Cath   We open the door . . .

Phil   Yes?

Cath   And there she is.

Phil   So there she is.

Cath   Then what?

Phil   I don't know. We say . . .

Cath   What do we say?

Phil   'Hello.'

Cath   Don't be silly.

Phil   We go . . .

He coughs terminally.

Cath   Sh!

He goes to open the door.

No!

Phil   No?

Cath   No . . . Or perhaps we should.

Phil   All right.

Cath   Go on.

Phil   Open it?

Cath   Open it!

Phil *puts his ear to the door.*

Phil (*whispers*)   I can hear her!

Cath (*whispers*)   You can't.

Phil (*whispers*)   I can!

He suddenly opens the door. **Pat** *is standing on the threshold. He automatically closes the door on her again in surprise, looks at* **Cath**, *then immediately reopens it.*

Phil   I'm sorry. I'd no idea. I was just, we were just . . .

Pat   Here . . .

She brings Eric's chair back in.

It's yours – it's not mine – I gave it to you. If you don't want it then that's your problem.

Cath   Oh, Pat . . .

She looks at **Phil**.

Pat   I don't want it. I hate the sight of it.

Phil   It's very nice of you . . .

Cath   We really are pleased to have it.

Phil   But what about Eric?

Pat   Eric?

Phil   Would he . . . want you to get rid of it?

Pat   I don't know, my loves. That's the wonderful thing. I didn't have to ask him.

Pat *goes out.* **Phil** *takes the chair back to the alcove.*

Phil   Yes?

Cath   Yes . . . Only . . .

Phil   What?

Cath   When she comes back?

Phil   She won't come back.

Cath   She will come back!

Phil   Not if we don't ask her up.

Cath   We didn't ask her up. She just came.

Phil   Then we don't ask her in.

Cath   Phil, be realistic.

Phil   Our piece of space. Yes? Our bit of world. We say.

Cath   Of course. Only if she comes to the door . . .

Phil   Then she stays at the door. All right?

Cath   All right. Only . . .

Phil   Decision. Yes? No Pat. No Eric.

He crams the chair back into the alcove.

No Eric's chair or Eric's old underpants.

He crams the various other items back in that fell out with the chair.

No Arthur . . . No Cyril . . . No coughs, no screams . . . No muddle . . . No mess . . . No *junk* . . .

He draws the curtain closed over everything.

Cath   But you don't mean no *children*. Do you? We'd like *children*.

Phil *turns in surprise.*

Phil   Children?

Everything comes tumbling out into the room again.

Cath   Wouldn't we?

Pause.

Phil   Cath, come here.

Cath   What?

Phil   Come here!

Pause. She goes across to him. He puts his arms round her.

Cath   What are you doing?

Phil   What do you mean, what am I doing? I'm putting my arms round you.

Cath   You're smelling my jumper.

Phil   I'm not smelling your jumper. I want to tell you something.

Cath   What?

Pause.

What?

Phil   I like it.

Cath   Like what?

Phil   Where the bed is.

Cath   You don't.

Phil   I do.

Cath   Yes, well . . .

Phil   I like *you.*

Cath   Do you?

He kisses her.

A bit?

Phil   A bit.

He kisses her.

Cath   We do want children, though, don't we?

Phil   Do we?

Cath   Don't we?

Phil   They might distract us.

Cath   From what?

Phil   From liking each other.

Cath   Do we like each other?

Phil   I've just said!

Cath   Have you?

Phil   I like you, I like you! How many times?

Cath   Don't you want to know whether I like you?

Phil   I know already.

Cath   Do you?

Phil   You mean you don't like me?

Cath   No.

Phil   Yes, you do.

Cath   No, I don't.

Phil   Don't be silly.

He kisses her.

Cath   You're a nasty old man.

Phil   I'm a nice old man.

He kisses her.

Cath   Always starting rows.

Phil   We don't have rows.

Cath   We do have rows.

Phil   No, we don't.

Cath   Yes, we do.

Phil   I hate having rows.

Cath   You love having rows.

Phil   I quite like having rows.

Cath   You're a nasty, pedantic, narrow-minded, quarrelsome, bullying old man.

Phil   Yes.

Cath   Yes!

Phil   *You* quite like having rows.

Cath   No, I don't.

Phil   Yes, you do.

He kisses her.

You do.

He kisses her.

Anyway, we don't really have rows, do we?

Cath   Don't we?

Phil   What do we have rows about?

Cath   Everything.

Phil   Everything?

Cath   The bed.

Phil   Oh, well, the bed.

Cath   The table. The chairs.

Phil   Not *this* chair.

Cath   Poor Pat.

Phil   Sob sob.

Cath   I ought to take her something in return . . .

She turns irresolutely towards the door. He pulls up the jumper he is wearing, and pulls it down over her head, so that she is inside it with him, her arms trapped, her head emerging from the top beside his.

Phil   Closer together. Yes?

Cath   All right.

Phil No more rows.

Cath No?

Phil We can't have rows inside the same jumper.

Cath Can't we?

Phil Not if we're doing everything together. Come on . . .

He pushes one of her feet forward with his.

Cath What are you doing?

Phil Whatever *you're* doing.

They begin to move about the room as one.

Cath Where are we going?

Phil Wherever we're going.

Cath Phil!

Phil One flesh. One heart . . .

Cath We'll fall over!

Phil One pair of legs.

They look at themselves in a mirror.

Cath One pair of heads.

Phil But side by side. Seeing everything from each other's point of view.

Cath Thinking downstairs we go.

They head towards the door.

Phil Thinking upstairs we stay.

They head away from the door.

Cath And upstairs we stay.

Phil One pair of hands.

They pick up Eric's chair.

Cath   Not picking up the chair.

Phil   Picking up the chair.

Cath   And putting it here.

They move it towards the space that she put it in before.

Phil   And putting it *here*.

They put it behind the curtain.

Cath   And putting it there.

Phil   You see how easy it is?

Cath   What?

Phil   Deciding where everything goes.

Cath   Did we decide?

Phil   We must have decided, if we did it.

Cath   So what are we deciding about children?

Phil   We're not deciding.

Cath   Aren't we?

Phil   Not now.

Cath   So when are we going to decide?

Phil   I don't know. We'll have to decide.

Cath   Decide when to decide?

Phil   Of course.

Cath   So when are we going to . . . ?

Phil   Decide when to decide? We'll have to decide.

Pause.

Cath   Perhaps we don't decide things.

Phil   Don't decide things?

Cath   Perhaps we just . . . do them.

Phil   All right, we'll do something else, and this time we'll watch ourselves in the mirror, and we'll see if we can see ourselves deciding. Yes?

Cath   All right.

They look at themselves in the mirror.

So what are we going to do?

Phil   That's what we're deciding.

They watch themselves.

Cath   Are we deciding now?

Phil   Yes, we're deciding now.

Pause.

We're gradually deciding . . .

*The jumper, and **Cath**'s jumper beneath it, slowly, sensuously begin to take themselves off, as they watch themselves intently in the mirror.*

Phil   Here it comes . . . It's a decision, a joint decision . . . Here it is . . . We've almost decided . . . It's like the sun coming up . . . It's just showing above the horizon now. Very bright. I'm going to sneeze . . .

The two jumpers envelope their heads, and then are lifted clear above them. They gaze at themselves in the mirror, smiling. Their arms come slowly down from above their heads, so that she is lying in his embrace.

Cath   I think we've decided.

She tilts her head back, so that her face dissolves into his.

Phil (*dreamily*)   And still we never saw it happen . . .

They sink slowly down on to the bed.

Curtain.

Act Two

The same.

But the furniture has been rearranged, and the austere order of the first act has become cluttered and confused. The pot-plant has grown. The toy dog has disappeared. A battered bicycle with one wheel missing is propped against the wall.

Scene One

Cath *is sitting at the table, working.* **Phil** *is sprawling back in the other chair, turned away from the table, holding a vacuum-cleaner and abstractedly picking his nose. He is wearing the same jumper as before, she is not. She suddenly looks up.*

Cath   What?

Phil *stops picking his nose.*

Phil   What?

Cath   I thought you said something.

Phil   No?

Cath   Oh.

She returns to her work. He returns to his thoughts and his nose. She glances round at him, then returns to her work. Pause. **Phil** *looks up at her.*

Phil   What?

Pause. **Cath** *works.*

Phil   I said 'what?'

Cath   What do you mean, 'what?'?

Phil   What do you mean, what do I mean? I mean 'what?'

Cath   I didn't say anything.

Phil   No.

Pause. Then **Cath** *suddenly looks up.*

Cath   What is all this?

Phil   What is all what?

Cath   All this 'What? What?' What are you talking about?

Phil   Nothing.

Cath   Nothing. Oh. That's interesting.

Phil   *I* said nothing. *You* said nothing. Nothing was said.

Pause. **Cath** *works.*

Cath   So why are you looking like that?

Phil   Why am I looking like *what?*

Cath   That.

Phil   This?

Cath   Yes.

Phil   I'm looking like this because this is what I look like.

Cath   No, it isn't.

Phil   Yes, it is.

Cath   You know perfectly well how you're looking.

Phil   I *don't* know how I'm looking. As a matter of fact. Human eyes being located where they are located. I know how *you're* looking. *You* don't know how you're looking. *You* know how *I'm* looking. *I* don't, though. All I know, since it's not a matter of observation but a matter of logic, is that whatever I'm looking like, I'm looking like it because it's what I look like.

Pause.

Also because of your saying 'what?' like that.

Cath   What?

Phil   Exactly.

Cath   I don't know what you're talking about. *I* said 'what?'? *You* said 'what?'

Phil   We both said 'what?'

Cath   So?

Phil   I didn't say it like that.

Cath   Like what?

Phil   Disingenuously.

Cath   What?

Phil   You see?

Cath   Just a moment. I said 'what' *disingenuously*?

Phil   Right.

Cath   How can anyone say 'what' *disingenuously*?

Phil   Very easily. By saying 'what?' when they don't mean 'what?' By saying 'what?' when they know perfectly well what had been said.

Cath   I haven't the slightest idea what you're talking about.

Pause.

Phil   Look, let's go right back to the beginning. Let's try to reconstruct this conversation before we've forgotten how it went. You said 'what?' . . .

Cath   *You* said 'what?'

Phil   You said it first.

Cath   Because you hadn't said anything!

Phil Exactly. Exactly! *I* said 'what?' because you said 'what?' when you knew perfectly well that I hadn't said anything. I said 'what?' as a genuine request for elucidation of your 'what?', because your 'what?' wasn't a genuine request for elucidation at all, since you knew that nothing had been said to elucidate.

Cath (*holds up her hand*) Phil. Stop. All right. This is about what it was about last time, is it?

Phil No? Why? What was it about last time?

Cath You know what it was about last time.

Phil I *don't* know what it was about last time.

Cath Really?

Phil No! I *don't*!

Pause.

Cath Honestly, you accuse *me* of being whatever it was.

Phil What did I accuse you of being?

Cath Your new word.

Phil My new word?

Cath You know what your new word is.

Phil What is my new word?

Pause.

Cath It's the word that describes your behaviour now, since you know perfectly well what the word is.

Phil And yours, since you do, too.

Pause. She works.

We used to talk.

Cath Did we?

Phil We used to sit here and something used to happen.

Cath What did we say?

Phil I can't remember.

Cath Lot of good *that* did, then.

Phil I used to enjoy it. Didn't you?

Cath Yes.

Pause.

Phil So what do you want me to say? 'I love you'?

Cath No, I've given up on that.

Phil I've just said it.

Cath Yes.

Phil What?

Cath Yes! Lovely!

Phil Not right?

Cath No – perfect. Thank you.

Phil I can't say it if you say.

Cath You can't say it if I say and you don't say it if I don't.

Phil No. Sad, isn't it.

Pause.

You don't notice I'm here half the time.

Cath I notice you picking your nose. You never used to pick your nose when I was here.

Phil Yes, I did.

Cath Only when I wasn't looking.

Phil If you weren't looking how did you know I was

picking my nose?

He gets up and takes the vacuum-cleaner to the kitchenette. She works.

Cath I don't need to look. I know what you're up to without looking.

Pause. He puts a saucepan over his head, and stands waiting for her to notice.

Anyway, half the time you're *not* here. You're in some world of your own.

Pause.

I know what you're doing now, by the way.

Pause. She glances up, then returns to work.

I knew it was something like that.

She folds up her books, and goes into the bathroom.

Phil (*from under the saucepan*) I'm looking for the soup. I can't see it.

The sound of taps running. **Phil** *takes the saucepan off his head and discovers that she has gone.*

(*Raises his voice.*) I thought there was some soup?

Pause. Louder.

Where's the soup?

Cath (*off*) In the bath.

Pause.

(*Off.*) Did you say what am I doing?

He shakes his head.

(*Off.*) Can't hear!

He expresses silent surprise and interest.

(*Off.*) I've told you before . . .

Phil   . . . you can't hear me when you've got the door shut.

The bathroom door opens, and **Cath** *appears.*

Cath   . . . I can't hear you when I've got the door shut! And don't say leave the door open, because I *can't* leave the door open, because if I leave the door open there isn't room to be in there!

She goes back into the bathroom.

Phil   I'm not saying Leave the door open . . .

Cath (*off*)   And don't say Then don't be in there!

Phil   I'm not saying Don't be in there . . .

Cath (*off*)   Because I've *got* to be in here if I'm going to have a bath . . . !

Phil   I'm not saying anything.

He goes to the alcove and draws the curtain back. It reveals not the confusion of the first act, but Eric's chair, neatly arranged at a small table covered with books and papers. He switches on a reading-lamp and sits down.

Cath (*off*)   Oh, really . . . ? Well, I'm not listening . . . ! Wasting your breath . . . La la la la la la la . . .

He pulls the curtain closed. She comes out of the bathroom.

Oh. Though why you're taking refuge in there I don't know, since I'm not in here, I'm in *there*!

She goes back into the bathroom. He looks out from behind the curtain.

Phil   Why don't you leave the door *half-open*?

The taps are turned off. She comes out of the bathroom, amazed.

Cath   Half-open?

Phil   Half-open. Yes! Wedge it half-open!

Cath   *Half-open?*

Phil   Half hyphen open.

Pause.

Cath   Half-open . . .

Phil   Half-open.

He closes the curtain again. She remains where she is.

Cath   Anyway, we both know what all this is really about.

Pause. He opens the curtain.

Phil   What is all this really about?

Cath   You know.

Phil   No?

Cath   Yes, you do.

Phil   I haven't the slightest idea.

Cath   I thought I wasn't supposed to say the word?

Phil   What word?

Cath   Theodore.

Pause. He closes the curtain.

Yes, well, I don't know how we can talk about it if I can't say the name. What's wrong with the name? I don't understand! Theodore . . . Anyway, *you're* the one who put him in there!

He opens the curtain.

Phil   *I* put him in there? *I* didn't put him in there.

Cath   You did!

He comes out of the alcove, pulls the toy dog out from some piece of furniture, and whacks it down on to the table.

Phil   *We* put it in there.

Cath   Oh. Yes. Well . . .

Phil   You're always doing this.

Cath   Always doing what?

Phil   Always saying *I* put things somewhere.

Cath   Well, you *did* put this particular thing somewhere!

Phil   No, I didn't. *We* did!

Pause.

We *did*! We *did*! You're always pretending it's me that makes the decisions.

Cath   Because it *is* you that makes the decisions.

Phil   It's *us* that make the decisions.

Pause.

Cath   I said If you want to put it in the thing, then put it in the thing.

Phil   Exactly. So then it's me that decided! That's exactly what I'm saying!

Cath   That you decided?

Phil   That you decided I decided!

Cath   What?

Phil   Look. I said, Do we want to put this thing in the thing?

Cath   No, *I* said, Do *you* want it in the thing?

Phil   Would you mind letting me finish?

Cath   Go on.

Phil   Thank you.

Cath It was exactly the same with the other thing.

Pause.

Phil Am I finishing what I'm saying or aren't I?

Cath Go on, then.

Phil I don't mind waiting while you bring up some other subject first. I just want to know which I'm doing.

Cath Yes. No. Fine. Get on with it.

Phil I'm finishing what I'm saying?

Cath Yes! Finish what you're saying!

Pause.

Phil What do you mean, it was exactly the same with the other thing? What other thing?

Cath Never mind. Go on.

Phil If you mean the bicycle . . .

Cath No, please. Let's not get back to the bicycle.

Phil It wasn't me that brought it up.

Cath What do you mean, it wasn't you that brought it up?

Phil I mean it wasn't me that brought it up!

Cath Last Saturday!

Pause.

Phil Up*stairs.*

Cath Upstairs, yes!

Phil Not up in the conversation.

Cath What?

Phil I didn't bring it up in the conversation.

Cath In the conversation? No, you brought it up in a

towering rage.

Phil   Anyway . . .

Cath   Anyway . . .

Pause.

Phil   *Our* bicycle, incidentally.

Cath   I *said* 'our bicycle'!

Phil   You said 'your bicycle'.

Cath   In fact I said 'the bicycle'.

Phil   You use it just as much as me.

Cath   Yes.

Phil   You *used* to use it just as much as me.

Cath   However . . .

Phil   When it had two wheels.

Cath   Let's not talk about the wheels.

Phil   No.

Cath   So.

Phil   So.

Pause.

In fact we both know perfectly well what this is all about.

Cath   That's what I said.

Phil   It happens every time I go in there.

Cath   Oh, you mean your little hidey-hole?

Phil   I mean my workspace.

Cath   I mean your workspace.

Phil   But I thought we'd *agreed*.

Cath Yes! Fine! Get right back in there and pull the curtain again!

Phil What we agreed, if you remember . . .

Cath I think it's completely mad!

Phil Yes, but what we agreed . . .

Cath But if you can't stand the sight of me then why don't you just move in there for good and never come out?

Phil What we agreed . . .

Cath You and Eric's chair together.

Phil What we agreed . . .

Cath I should have thought it was a little bit *inauthentic*.

Phil A little bit what?

Cath Inauthentic. Oh, you've forgotten about 'inauthentic'. How about the *natural order*?

Phil What natural order?

Cath The natural order of the universe.

Phil I don't know what you're talking about.

Cath No.

Phil What we agreed . . .

Pause.

Cath Go on, then!

Phil Is that we both needed our own . . . micro-climate.

Pause.

Yes?

Cath Our own micro-climate?

Phil   Our own corner. Our own piece of the universe.

Cath   Where's my piece of the universe?

Phil   The bathroom!

Cath   The bathroom? *You* use the bathroom!

Phil   Yes, and you're perfectly welcome to borrow my workspace!

Cath   You mean sit behind that curtain? I think hiding yourself away behind that curtain is absolutely mad! You might just as well put your head back inside that saucepan!

Pause.

Phil   Anyway, the relevant fact is that we agreed. Yes? Just as we also agreed about the bicycle.

Cath   We didn't agree about the bicycle.

Phil   We agreed that it couldn't stay out on the pavement, because if it did then the other wheel would go as well. Yes?

Cath   I agreed that it couldn't stay on the *pavement* . . .

Phil   You agreed that it couldn't stay on the *pavement*. Yes. You also agreed . . . .

Cath   I didn't agree to keep it in here!

Phil   You also agreed that it couldn't go in the hall downstairs, or else Pat would fall over it and break her leg, and then she wouldn't be able to come up here and drop in on us at all hours of the day and night, which would be a tragic loss to both of us.

Cath   I didn't agree to keep it in here, though!

Phil   But there isn't anywhere else!

Cath   So?

Phil   So, logically . . .

Cath I thought we agreed you weren't going to say 'logically'?

Phil Logically . . .

Cath Let's forget the bicycle.

Phil Logically we must have agreed it was coming in here.

Cath Yes, yes, yes. Fine. Wonderful. Just so long as it's not in *my* bit.

Phil All right. Just so long as you agree that we did agree . . .

Cath Yes. I've said. Yes. So you go back in there, I'll go back in there . . .

She goes to the bathroom. He has not moved.

Now what?

Phil *Your* bit? What do you mean, *your* bit?

Cath Round my side of the bed.

Phil Oh, that's *your* bit, is it?

Cath *Now* what's going on?

Phil I didn't know you had a special bit of the room.

Cath It's not special. It's simply my side of the bed. What's wrong with that?

Phil When was this decided?

Cath It wasn't decided. It's always been my side of the bed.

Phil Always been your side of the bed?

Cath I thought so.

Phil I didn't know that.

Cath What do you mean, you didn't know that?

Phil   I mean I didn't know that.

Cath   It's my piece of the universe.

Phil   Not in *here*!

Cath   Why not?

Phil   This is us! That's the point!

He indicates the bathroom, the alcove, and the room they are in.

You. Me. Us!

Cath   You've got your bit of the room.

Phil   No, I haven't.

Cath   Yes, you have.

Phil   Where?

Cath   Round your side of the bed.

Phil   This? I don't think of this as my bit.

Cath   Yes, you do.

Phil   I *do* think of it as my bit?

Cath   Of course you do.

Phil   How do you know what I think?

Cath   Because if you find anything of mine there you shout 'What's this thing doing round my side of the bed?'

Pause.

Phil   So where does your bit stop?

Cath   Here.

Phil   Here. There's a line, is there?

Cath   We don't need a line. We both know.

Phil   Oh, we both know, do we?

Cath   Of course we know.

Phil   You mean *you* know?

Cath   I mean we both know.

Phil   You keep telling me what I know!

Cath   Because you don't seem to know.

Phil   I don't know what I know?

Cath *goes back towards the bathroom.*

Cath   I'm going to have my bath.

Phil (*stops her*)   Let me just get this straight. All this is yours? Yes? Over this piece of floor here you have absolute sovereignty. And the boundary of your territory is an imaginary line extending from the foot of the bed. While all *this*, up to an imaginary line from the foot of the bed on this side, is mine, to have and to hold at my own good pleasure, to lease out, sell, burn, put to pasture or develop as building plots, at my own absolute discretion.

Cath   Phil, why are you behaving like this?

Phil   I'm not behaving like anything. I'm trying, in an absolutely uncontentious way, to codify what seems to have become accepted practice, so that we both know where we stand. Now, these two areas apart, is all the rest of the room subject to mutual agreement or not?

Cath   As far as *I* know.

Phil   As far as *you* know. Good.

Cath   Well, *isn't* it?

Phil   As far as *I* know, yes. Though whether I know how far I know . . .

Cath   Let's just say yes. Yes, it is.

Phil   Yes. All right. Yes?

Cath Yes.

Pause.

Just so long as no more things suddenly vanish into things.

Phil Cath, for the last time!

He snatches up the toy dog.

It wasn't *me* who put this thing in the thing!

Cath I know. It was *us*. It's not *you* waving it around. *Us* waving it around. Not *my* face we're waving it in. *Our* face.

Phil You *don't* want to talk sensibly – we *won't* talk.

He throws the dog down, returns to the alcove, and draws the curtain. Pause. **Cath** *picks up the dog and strokes it. Pause. Then abruptly she goes out of the front door. Pause.* **Phil** *opens the curtain and looks out. He reluctantly emerges and crosses to the bathroom door.*

Phil Sorry.

Pause. Louder.

Sorry!

Pause.

Cath . . . ?

Pause.

You haven't got the taps on, don't pretend you can't hear . . . I've said I'm sorry . . .

Pause.

I know you're listening – I can hear you . . . I can hear you *listening*. – Yes – How can I hear you listening? – I have very sharp ears.

Pause.

You're always saying *I* sulk, *I* won't make up
quarrels . . .

Pause.

Cath . . . I love you . . . Yes . . . ? Cath, I've said it!
What do you want me to do?

Pause.

I do, actually, Cath. I do love you. I love you very
much . . . I don't know how else to say it . . .

Pause. **Cath** *pushes open the front door, and stops at the sight of
him.*

Phil   I'm just standing here talking to myself, am I?

Cath   Apparently.

Pause.

Phil   Oh. Very clever.

Cath   What?

Phil   You were listening, were you?

Cath   Listening? No? Listening to what?

Phil   Nothing.

Cath   Listening to nothing?

Phil   Never mind.

Cath   Why, what were you saying?

Phil   Nothing at all.

Cath   Something I wasn't supposed to hear?

Phil   No.

Cath   No you weren't? Or no I wasn't?

Phil   I'm not going to say it again.

Cath   Not going to say what again?

Phil   Nothing.

Pause.

Cath   Oh.

She goes to the bathroom.

Phil   Cath!

Cath   What?

Pause.

What?

Phil   How's it all got like this? It didn't use to be like this!

Cath   Didn't it?

Phil   No!

Cath   I can't remember.

Phil   Cath!

Cath   Well . . . things change.

Phil   What things?

Cath   Things.

Phil   You mean me?

Cath   No.

Phil   You?

Cath   Possibly.

Phil   You haven't changed.

Cath   Haven't I?

Phil   Have you?

Cath   I don't know.

Phil   I'll tell you what's changed. It's not me. It's not you. It's us.

Cath   No!

Phil   No?

Cath   Don't say things like that.

Phil   If they're true . . .

Cath   Don't say them.

Phil   No . . .

Cath   Anyway, it's this place.

Phil   What – changed?

Cath   No, *not* changed! *Not* changed, that's the trouble! It's all this! And this! And this!

Phil   I thought you liked this place?

Cath   I do!

Phil   You used to like it.

Cath   I do like it! I just want to . . .

Phil   What?

Cath   Get out of here!

Phil   Move?

Cath   Not move.

Phil   Go away?

Cath   For a bit. Yes? Get right away from it all.

Phil   All right. The question is when.

Cath   When?

Phil   When we can get away.

Cath   Now!

Phil   What – this week?

Cath No! Now!

She opens the door.

Come on!

Phil Cath, don't start being all like that.

Cath Like what?

Phil All Now here we are at the South Pole.

Cath No, but we can just walk out of the door.

Phil Except we can't.

Cath Why not?

Phil We've got things to do.

Cath Forget them.

Phil Your thing.

Cath What thing?

Phil I don't know. Your great thing tomorrow.

Cath Oh, that.

Phil You see?

Cath We'll forget about it. Come on! Off we go.

She waits, holding the door open.

Phil (*reluctantly*) We could go for a walk.

Cath We could go anywhere.

Phil Where's anywhere?

Cath Anywhere we like.

Phil We can't go *anywhere*. We've got to go *somewhere*.

Cath China?

Phil Cath!

Cath That's somewhere.

Phil Yes.

Cath Bournemouth.

Pause.

Phil (*reluctantly*) We could go to your mother's . . .

Cath Anywhere.

Phil Anywhere. All right. How about . . . here?

Cath Here?

Phil Here's anywhere.

Pause.

Cath Here . . .

She closes the door.

All right. Here.

Phil Do you mind?

Cath Not at all.

Phil Even if we'd gone somewhere else, it would still have been here when we'd got there.

Cath Yes. So, here we are.

Phil Here we are.

She looks round the room.

Cath What do you think?

Phil What?

Cath Quite nice. Rather like home. Have we got a view?

She looks out of the window.

Phil No South Pole business, though, Cath.

Cath Why not? We're on holiday . . . Bit of a view.

Phil   Let's just *be*. All right?

Cath   Bathroom?

Phil   Cath!

She looks into the bathroom.

Cath   Yes. They've even run the bath for us.

Phil   It's just so exhausting when you start this kind of thing.

He hurls himself down on to the bed.

Cath   What's the bed like?

Phil   I'm not playing.

She sits down on one of the chairs. Pause.

What are you doing now?

Cath   Nothing.

Phil   Nothing. Good.

Cath   Having a holiday. Relaxing. Watching the world go by.

Pause.

Why? What are you doing?

Phil   Nothing.

Cath   Relaxing?

Phil   No.

Cath   Not relaxing?

Phil   No.

Cath   Close your eyes.

Phil   I don't want to close my eyes. I don't want to do anything.

Cath   So what are you looking at?

Phil   The ceiling.

Cath   What's it like?

Phil   What's it like? The ceiling? It's not like anything.

Cath   Not like a ceiling?

Pause.

Phil   Yes, it's like a ceiling. That's exactly what it's like. A ceiling.

Pause.

Cath   Any frescoes on it?

Phil   Cath . . .

Cath   What?

Phil   Don't.

Pause.

Cath   Not overdoing it, are you?

Phil   What?

Cath   Not getting too much sun?

Pause.

Phil   I'm not getting too much sun, no.

Cath   Or bitten by anything?

Pause.

Phil   Not bitten.

Cath   Perfect place.

Phil   Cath, I'm so miserable!

Pause.

Cath   Phil . . .

Phil   Nothing else!

Cath I love you.

Pause.

Phil I know.

Cath Oh, you know?

Phil You know I know.

Cath How do you know?

Phil I just do.

Cath Because I say it.

Phil Because you don't need to say it.

Pause.

Anyway *I* said it.

Cath Said what?

Phil The converse.

Cath When?

Phil You weren't here.

Cath You said it when I wasn't here?

Phil I didn't know you weren't here.

Cath You mean you didn't notice?

Pause.

Oh. Then. So what did you say?

Phil You know what I said.

Cath Go on.

Phil Not now you've asked me to.

He turns away from her, on to his side. Pause.

Cath Anyway, there's some soup.

Pause.

It's in the thing.

Pause.

Phil I'm busy.

Cath Why, what are you doing?

Phil I'm watching the clock.

Cath That must be interesting.

Phil It is, actually.

Pause.

Cath What's interesting about it?

Phil The second hand. The way it goes round.

Pause.

Cath Why, how does it go round?

Phil Quite slowly. But very steadily. Down . . . down . . . Under . . . Up the other side . . . Actually, this is fascinating.

He sits up, interested, and picks up the clock.

Round it comes again . . . Look, look!

He gets up and puts the clock on the table, then sits down beside her.

You see?

Cath Yes.

Phil You're not looking.

Cath I looked.

Phil You have to keep looking.

Cath Lovely.

Phil Keep your eyes on it.

Cath Anyway, I've got work to do. I've got my thing

tomorrow.

She gets up, then stands fascinated by the clock in spite of herself.

Phil   I've got a thing tomorrow. That doesn't stop me doing things today . . . On it goes. On and on. Taking it as it comes. A moment at a time. Living every minute to the full.

Cath   *You've* got a thing tomorrow? You haven't got a thing tomorrow.

Phil   I've got a thing tomorrow.

Cath   I don't know what you're talking about.

Pause. They both watch the clock.

Phil   You see? Down . . . down . . . Nice and slow.

She sits down again.

Cath   I don't call that slow.

Phil   Slow and steady.

Cath   It's fast. I call that fast.

Phil   Still coming down . . . Not halfway round yet . . .

Cath   It is now.

Phil   Oh, *now* it is.

Cath   Now it's past halfway.

Phil   It's on the seven.

Cath   It's past the seven . . . It's nearly on the eight . . .

Phil   It's on the eight.

Cath   It's past the eight . . .

Phil   Up it goes. Up . . . up . . .

Cath   You can't take it in. It keeps changing. Every time you think you know where it is it's somewhere else.

Phil   Ten . . .

Cath   Close your eyes!

Phil   Closing our eyes won't stop it.

Cath   Yes, it will. Now, when I say 'open', open them. Yes? And when I say 'shut', shut them. All right?

Phil   You're being all like that again.

Cath   Ready?

Phil   No.

Cath   Open. Shut.

Phil   I wasn't ready.

Cath   Open. Shut.

Phil   I can't shut them before I've got them open!

Cath   Open. Shut.

Phil   We'll both say it! Ready?

Phil } *(together)*   Open. Shut.
Cath }

Phil   Again.

Phil } *(together)*   Open. Shut.
Cath }

Cath   You see?

Phil   See what?

Cath   We caught it!

Phil   Caught what?

Cath   The thing. We caught it not moving!

Phil   Oh, the thing.

Cath   You weren't looking at the thing?

Phil   I was looking at you.

Cath   Oh. Was *I* moving?

Phil   No.

Cath   What was I doing?

Phil   Nothing. You were just... Hold on, I'll do it again. You were just ... Open. Shut ... Just *there*.

Cath   Just *there*?

Phil   Do it to me. We'll do it to each other. Eyes closed ...

Cath   What are we trying to do?

Phil   To get hold of it all for a moment. To see what we're like *now*.

Cath   Now?

Phil   *Now*!

Cath   Are we saying 'now' or are we saying 'open'?

Phil   We're saying 'now'.

Cath   'Now.' Right.

Phil   We'll say it together.

Phil ⎫
         ⎬   (*together*)   *Now*!
Cath ⎭

Phil   Brilliant!

They both open their eyes permanently.

Cath   You had your eyes wide open!

Phil   So did you! And your mouth!

Cath   Yes! You had your mouth open!

Phil   We'll always remember that.

Cath   When we're very old.

Phil   And everything's got mixed up in our memory and run together with everything else . . .

Cath   And we can't remember what anything was like . . .

Phil   We'll remember that once . . .

Cath   Once . . .

Phil   At one particular moment in time . . .

Cath   It was now . . .

Phil   Precisely now, and we were precisely like that.

Cath   Yes. And we'll remember all the things we were thinking at that particular moment, all the things we were feeling.

Phil   Yes! No. What things we were thinking?

Cath   Well, whatever it was.

Phil   We weren't thinking anything. *Nothing* was happening. It was one instant. Everything was fixed. That's the point.

Cath   *I* was thinking.

Phil   Not in that *instant*, you weren't.

Cath   Yes, I was.

Phil   You couldn't have been.

Cath   I *was*! I know *you* weren't.

Phil   No, because I couldn't. By the time I'd have thought 'I' the instant would have been over. There wouldn't have been time to get on to the 'love', never mind the 'you'.

Cath   No.

Phil   Well, there wouldn't.

Cath   No.

Phil   What you mean is that you thought it just afterwards.

Cath   You don't know what I mean.

Phil   I know what you *don't* mean.

Cath   And you don't know what I was thinking.

Phil   I know what you *weren't* thinking, because I know what you *can't* have been thinking, and I know you *can't* have been thinking it because it was impossible.

Cath   Logically?

Phil   Logically, yes.

Pause. She laughs.

What?

Cath   Nothing.

She sits astride his lap.

Phil   What's all this?

She moves her hands slowly down over his body.

Cath, what's going on?

Cath   What do you mean, what's going on?

Phil   I mean, what's going on?

Cath   You know what's going on.

Phil   I don't, actually.

Cath   Don't you? Some of you does.

Phil   Some of me?

Cath   This bit.

Phil   Maybe it's jumping to conclusions.

Cath   Yes. Or lying.

Phil   Anyway, it's only doing that because you're

making it.

Cath I'm saying Say it?

Phil Exactly.

Cath Oh. So your response is ... inauthentic? Disingenuous? Indeterminate?

Pause.

Phil No, it's logically compelling.

He pulls his jumper over her head.

A knock at the door.

Pat (*off*) Cath ...

Their heads emerge from the top of the jumper, looking in the direction of the door.

(*Off.*) Cath?

Phil (*whispers*) She listens! She waits outside that door and listens!

Cath (*whispers*) No, it's my fault ...

Phil (*whispers*) Oh, no! You went down?

Cath (*whispers*) You were behind the thing!

Phil (*whispers*) And you told her to come up?

Cath (*whispers*) I was going *there*! But she was busy!

Phil (*whispers*) So you said 'Come up'?

Pat (*off*) Cath ... ?

Cath Coming!

She extracts herself from the jumper.

Phil (*whispers*) But we *agreed*!

Cath (*whispers*) I'll get rid of her.

Pat (*off*) Cath, I'll come back.

Cath   Hold on!

She goes to the door. He retires to the alcove.

(*Whispers.*) You're not . . . ?

Phil (*whispers*)   I am.

Cath (*whispers*)   You can't!

Phil (*whispers*)   I can.

He closes the curtain. She opens the door.

Pat   What – trouble?

Cath   No. Come in.

Pat *comes uncertainly in.*

Pat   Only I don't want to come up if it's the wrong moment . . .

Cath   It's not. Sit down.

Pat   He's out, is he?

Cath   No. Tea? Coffee?

Pat   Not for me, love.

She sits down.

What, he's in the . . . ?

She nods at the bathroom.

Cath   No, no.

Pat   Oh, sorry. Only I thought . . .

Cath   Of course.

Pat *looks round the room. She lowers her voice.*

Pat   He's not behind the . . . ?

Cath   Yes.

Pat   Oh, I see.

Pause.

Cath   Phil?

Pause.

Phil!

Pat   Yes, well, don't bother him, Cath.

Cath   Phil!

Pat *stands up.*

Pat   I'll come back another time.

Cath   Sit down.

Pat   He's got things to do.

Cath   Has he?

Pat   You've both got things to do, I know that.

Cath   No, no.

Pat   I wouldn't have come, only you said . . .

Cath   Yes!

Pat   And I thought Lovely, and then I thought No,
hold on, don't rush at it, I know Phil doesn't want me
up there all the time . . .

Cath   Don't be silly.

Pat   And now of course things have moved on, I know
how it is . . .

Cath   Just sit down. Don't take any notice.

Pat *sits down at the table.* **Cath** *sits opposite her. Pause.*

Pat   Eric was like that. He'd go all quiet, not a word
out of him. He'd come up here, you know. Get away
from me. Then nothing. Just cough cough.

Cath   Yes, Phil thinks we all have to have our own
personal micro-climate. (*Louder.*) Micro-climate – yes?

They both look at the curtain. No response.

Pat   Well, you've got to get out of each other's way,
Cath. I don't know where *you* go off to.

Cath   Me? Nowhere.

Phil (*off*)   The bathroom.

Cath   Oh, yes, the bathroom. The bathroom's me.
Except when he's using it, which is at least as often as
me. And then I have this piece of floor here, running
up to an imaginary line extending from the foot of the
bed.

Pat   No, but you do, don't you. You divide things up.

Cath   This is him, here, up to an imaginary line on
this side of the bed.

Pat   I was the windows. Anything to do with the
windows – that was me. He always blamed me for the
windows. So that was *my* fault, of course, when the sash
broke, and the window came down on top of him.

Cath   *He's* the windows. I'm the curtains.

Pat   No, I was always the windows. Windows and
door-handles. And the roof. And the fireplaces. Because
he liked modern, you see, Eric. He was always for
modern. So anything that wasn't modern in the house,
and it went wrong, that was my fault. He'd sit there
reading his paper and I'd know something was up just
from the look on his face. So I wouldn't say anything –
I wouldn't give him the satisfaction. I'd wait. He'd go
on reading the paper, not a word, just this tight little
look, and I'd know he'd got this wonderful grievance.
I'd wait. *He'd* wait. Then just as I was going out of the
room, say, just as I was putting the supper on the table,
out it would bounce. 'The bedroom door-handle,' he'd
say. It used to make me so cross! 'The bedroom door-
handle.' Like that. As soon as he said it I could feel my
muscles all clench up. I'd just stop where I was, look at

him, wait, not say anything. 'It's loose, it's going to
come off,' he'd say. And so pleased with himself! Always
knew I'd got a bad character, and now here I was,
caught in the act, letting the bedroom door-handle get
loose. So of course I wouldn't admit it. Nothing to do
with me! 'Oh,' I'd say, 'is it really? Then why don't you
get upstairs and mend it?' But inside, Cath, inside, I
knew he was right, I knew it was me that had done it,
because if it was the door-handle then it had to be me.
So he wouldn't mend it, and I wouldn't get Mr Weeks
to do it, and he'd sigh and raise his eyebrows every time
he put his hand on it, and not say anything, and I'd
look the other way, and not say anything, until in the
end it'd fall off, and then at last, with a special holy
look like Jesus picking up the cross, he'd get the toolbox
out, and there wouldn't be any screws in the tin, so he'd
have to do it with three nails and some glue instead,
and there'd be blood dripping on the carpet, only he
wouldn't let me put a plaster on it for him, and then I
couldn't tell Mr Weeks about it when he came to do the
boiler because that'd look as if I was criticising his
handiwork and turning up my nose at the great sacrifice
he'd made even though he was in the right and I was in
the wrong.

Pause.

The boiler, that was me as well.

Cath I'm the soap, I don't know why.

Pat The boiler, the drain outside the back door. Yes, I
don't know why I was the drain.

Cath The soap and the towels.

Pat But then *he* was the lights and the washing-
machine. Oh yes. All the machines, all the electrical.
Anything modern, you see. He'd come home in the
evening – darkness. 'That washing-machine,' I'd say
before he could so much as open his mouth. 'You'll

have to do something about it, Eric. Water all over the
floor. Flash! Crack! I wonder it didn't kill me.' And at
once he'd go mad. 'There's nothing wrong with the
machine,' he'd say. 'It's what you ask it to do.' Shouting
away at me. Because he knew it was his fault, you see,
the washing-machine. If it was a gadget, if it was labour-
saving, then that was his responsibility. Poor Eric. Poor
old boy. But you can't take the blame for everything,
can you, Cath. You've got to divide things up.

Cath My relations.

Pat Oh, relations, yes. All down to you. All *his*
relations.

Cath All our friends.

Pat People. Other people. That's all your side of the
business.

Cath 'You haven't invited so-and-so round again?'

Pat That's me, is it?

Cath Not you. No.

Pat I bet it is. You'd be down to me if Eric was here.

Pause.

Is he all right behind there?

Cath I expect so.

Pat We're not disturbing him?

Cath No. He's disturbing us.

Pause.

Pat Anything to do with strikes, trains not running,
traffic-jams, that kind of thing, that was modern, that
was Eric's fault. Football hooligans. Russia. Oh, yes, he
was always Labour. America. Yes, well – modern again.

Pause.

Yes, and it was the same with the children. Oh, all
kinds of things you're going to find out about each other
as soon as there are three of you. You'll be off out of
here by then, though. I'll have two more faces in here.
Two more strangers.

Pause.

Cath (*sharply*) Phil!

Pause.

Pat I must be getting back, Cath.

She rises.

Cath Sit down.

Pat I've got the washing-machine on . . .

Cath Sit down!

Pat *sits. Pause.* **Pat** *sees the toy dog.*

Pat Oh, and Theodore's come out again! He used to
be up there, do you remember?

Cath Yes.

Pat Been everywhere, that dog. In, out, up, down.
Wonderful, the use you've got out of him.

Cath Wonderful.

Pat I remember when you first arrived. You didn't
have anything! Just you and the walls. Now look at you.

Cath Yes.

Pat Here you are.

Cath Here we are.

Pause.

I'm sorry.

Pat *We'd* have rows. Eric and me. He'd get so angry!

The angrier he got the less he'd say. The less he said
the more I said. The more I said the angrier he got.
Round and round. Up and down. Back and forth. Soon
as it stops – up it starts again. Then afterwards – you
can't even remember what it was all about.

Cath What was the rest of it about?

Pat What rest of it?

Cath When you weren't having rows.

Pause.

Pat I can't remember. Just there it was.

Cath Yes.

Pat There it was. Then there it wasn't. It doesn't last
long, I'll tell you that, whatever it's like.

She goes to the front door.

One moment it's there, and it's there for ever. Next
moment ... (*Calls.*) I'll say goodbye, then, Phil!

She waits. **Cath** *turns to look at the alcove.*

Cath Phil! (*To* **Pat**.) Wait a moment ...

But **Pat** *has gone.* **Cath** *closes the door, then sits down at the
table and picks up the clock.*

Cath You can come out. She's gone.

Pause.

And I *was* thinking it, you know. When we looked at
each other. I'll tell you how I know I was thinking it.
Because I think it all the time. I don't have to think the
words, one by one. The thought's just in my mind,
complete, every moment of the day. Even now.
Especially now ... Over the top again. Another minute
gone ... I know what you're doing behind that curtain.
You're thinking 'Shall I come out?' 'No,' you're
thinking, 'I'd better sulk for a bit longer. Then I'll come

out, and I won't say anything, but I'll give her a little kiss on the back of her neck, and I'll put the soup on the table, and we'll eat, and we'll talk, and we'll go to bed, and we'll put our arms round each other, and everything will be all right.'

She looks at the clock.

It's still *now* . . . Now . . . Now . . . More now . . . Or perhaps you're thinking something else altogether. I don't know. Perhaps you're not thinking. Not breathing . . . I don't know, do I, if I can't see you . . . Can't touch you, can't hear you . . . I don't even know if you exist . . . Not *logically.* Do I . . . ? Perhaps you don't exist. Perhaps you never did exist . . . Phil . . . ? Love . . . ?

She goes to the curtain across the alcove.

Come on, I'm going to open the curtain . . . Phil . . . ?

She pulls the curtain back. Pause.

Where are you? Phil! What's happened? Phil, come on! Don't be silly . . .

Pause.

You're not hiding in the curtain . . . ?

She pulls the curtain closed. Pause. She is very distressed.

Phil! Where are you? Please! Phil!

The sound of the curtain being opened. She gasps.

Phil   Did you say soup?

Pause.

Cath   Where were you?

Phil   Nowhere. Here. Soup?

Cath   Soup. Yes.

Phil   What?

Cath   Nothing.

Phil   In the thing?

Cath   In the thing.

He picks up the toy dog, tosses it behind the curtain, then crosses to the kitchenette and starts to heat the soup.

Blackout.

Scene Two

Half the pictures are off the wall, half the books off the shelves, stacked ready for moving. Half the contents of the room have either already gone, or are in plastic bin-liners. **Cath** *is throwing things into a bin-liner.* **Phil** *is standing holding the pillows.*

Cath   What?

Phil   Nothing. Just looking.

Cath   Looking at what?

Phil   All this.

Cath   Rubbish.

Phil   Rubbish?

Cath   This.

She drags the bin-liner to the door, and continues to work.

You're not going to just stand there, are you?

Phil   I'm not just standing there.

Cath   You're not *doing* anything.

Phil   I *am* doing something.

Cath   Carry some stuff down to the van.

Phil   I'm feeling.

Cath   Feeling? Feeling what?

Phil   You know . . . Just a bit . . . Well . . .

Cath   Oh. Yes. Bed.

She starts to strip the bed.

Phil   I mean, just a bit. Aren't you?

Cath   Yes. Come on.

He puts the pillows into the rubbish-bag.

Phil   You're not.

Cath   I am. Bed, bed!

He helps her strip the bed.

Phil   Remember the snowstorm?

Cath   What did you do with the pillows?

Phil   Bag. And we were rolling off the edge of the world?

Cath   That's rubbish!

She takes the pillows out of the rubbish-bag and transfers them to another bin-liner.

Phil   And Pat came in?

She indicates different bin-liners.

Cath   Rubbish . . . Bedroom . . . Living-room . . . Right?

Phil   Right. She thought I was murdering you. Do you remember that?

Cath   Yes. Up . . .

They up-end the mattress.

Phil   Heartbreaking.

Cath   What's the matter?

Phil   It took us two years to get it there.

Cath   Ready?

Phil   First we had it *there*. No, first we had it *there*! I'd forgotten that.

Cath   Lift . . .

Phil   Now where is it?

Cath   Move . . .

They carry the mattress to the door.

Phil   Nowhere.

Cath   Mind the thing.

Phil   So slow to put things together . . .

They carry the mattress out.

(*Off.*) Down the stairs?

Cath (*off*)   Over the bannisters.

Phil (*off*)   Over the bannisters?

Cath (*off*)   Quicker.

The sound of the mattress falling down the stairwell. They reappear.

Phil   So quick to blow them all to bits again . . .

He looks back at the door, hand to mouth.

Pat!

Cath   She went to the corner. Get that thing out of the way.

She indicates the plant.

Phil   You remember the size it was when we bought it?

Cath   Yes.

He starts to slide it towards the door, while she goes on clearing the room.

Phil You wanted to put it in the corner there.

Cath Anyway, it'll get plenty of light in the new living-room.

He stops work.

Phil The living-room?

Cath Presumably.

Phil Oh.

Cath It's not going in the bedroom?

Phil Isn't it?

Cath Is it?

Phil It's always *been* in the bedroom.

Cath What, this? This wasn't the bedroom.

Phil This wasn't the bedroom?

Cath Yes, well, now we've got a living-room *and* a bedroom we've got to decide about things.

Phil So what are you saying?

Cath What do you mean, what am I saying? I'm saying get the plant out of here before someone falls over it.

Phil You're saying you don't like it?

Cath I love it!

Phil You don't.

Cath All right, I don't.

Phil You *don't* like it?

Cath I just don't want it in my bedroom.

Phil *Your* bedroom?

Cath *The* bedroom.

Phil   *Our* bedroom.

She holds up something.

Cath   This thing?

Phil   Cath, we're not going to let it take over, are we, having a bedroom and a living-room? We're not going to let it change us?

Cath   No. Do we want to keep it?

Phil   No.

She dumps it in the rubbish-bag.

Yes.

Cath   Make up your mind.

She takes it out of the rubbish-bag.

Phil   Make up *my* mind?

Cath   Make up *our* mind.

Phil   Right.

Cath   No.

She dumps it in the rubbish-bag.

Phil   Cath, what is all this?

Cath   What is all what?

Phil   All this great thing.

Cath   I just want to get on, get out of here.

Phil   Get out of here?

Cath   Now we're going.

Phil   I thought you liked this place.

Cath   So you keep saying.

Phil   And you don't?

Cath I *did*.

Phil *Did?*

Cath Come on! We've got to get things done!

They begin sliding the plant out of the room.

Phil So when did you stop liking the *plant?*

Cath I've never liked it.

Phil *Never* liked it?

He stops work.

Cath Not much, no.

Phil Not when we bought it?

Cath No.

Phil We bought it together! We chose it together!

Cath *You* chose it.

She drags the plant out single-handed. He follows her out.

Phil (*off*) What are you saying?

Cath (*off*) Don't keep saying what am I saying! I'm saying what I'm saying!

She comes back in, and sets to work on the pictures. He follows her back in.

Phil You said you liked it.

Cath When?

Phil When we bought it.

Cath Did I?

Phil Why did you say you liked it if you didn't?

Cath No idea. Are we taking this?

She holds up one of the pictures.

Phil   Are we taking *that*? What's happening?

Cath   Yes or no?

Phil   You don't like *that*, either?

Cath   I love it.

Phil   I don't understand . . .

Cath   You want it?

Phil   *I* want it.

Cath   Then we're taking it.

She puts it and other pictures outside the door.

Phil   How about the table?

Cath   Table. Right.

She picks up one end, and waits for him to pick up the other.

Phil   You want to take it?

Cath   Do I want to take the *table*?

Phil   Yes.

Cath   Don't mess around.

Phil   No, I'm asking you.

Cath   Yes. I want to take the table.

Phil   You like the table?

Cath   I can't lift it on my own.

Phil   I want to know.

Pause.

Cath   Do I like the *table*?

Phil   Yes. Do you like the table?

Pause.

Cath   Look, we've got to *clean* the place . . .

Phil No, this is important.

Pause.

Cath You want me to tell you truthfully whether I like the table?

Phil I want you to tell me truthfully whether you like the table.

Pause. She looks at it.

Cath I don't know whether I like the table.

Phil You don't know whether you like the table?

Cath What do you want me to say?

Phil I want you to say what you want to say.

Cath It's a table.

Phil Oh. Right. Thank you.

Cath Right?

Phil Right. It's a table.

They pick the table up and carry it out.

Cath (*off*) Mind!

Phil (*off*) What?

A splintering sound, off.

Cath (*off*) I said Mind!

Phil (*off*) What does it matter?

They reappear.

It's only a table. Chairs?

Cath *You* take the chairs.

She gives him the two original chairs.

Phil And as far as you're concerned they're just . . . chairs?

Cath Yes. Throw *them* down the stairs as well.

He takes the chairs out.

Anyway, you're the one who doesn't like the chairs.

He comes back.

Phil *I* don't like the chairs?

Cath You don't like Eric's chair.

She hands it to him.

Phil I don't like Eric's chair?

Cath Well, you don't.

Phil I sit on it!

Cath You never *did* like it.

Phil When didn't I like it?

Cath You've forgotten.

Phil I haven't forgotten.

Cath You never remember when you've changed your mind about something.

Phil I haven't changed my mind.

Cath You're always changing your mind.

Phil What?

She takes the chair out of his hands and puts it outside.

Cath (*off*) You didn't like this place for a start.

Phil What do you mean, I didn't like this place?

Cath (*off*) You walked through this door . . .

She comes in.

You took one look round . . .

She looks round. The room is now almost as empty as when they first saw it.

And you said No.

Phil   No, I didn't.

Cath   You said it twice. You said it three times. 'No. No. No!'

Phil   I said What do you think?

Cath   You were standing here. I remember.

Phil   I was standing *here.*

Cath   'No. No. No.'

Phil   'What do you think?'

Cath   'No. No. No.' You told Pat we didn't want it!

Phil   'What do you think?' That's what I said! I was standing exactly *here*!

Cath   Yes, and what did *I* say?

Phil   What did *you* say? I'll tell you what you said. You said No. No, no, no.

Cath   I said What do *you* think?

Phil   I said Yes.

Cath   You said No.

Phil   I said Yes.

Cath   All right, you said Yes.

She pulls out the vacuum-cleaner from behind the curtain, and hands it to him while she plugs it in.

Phil   I did.

Cath   Yes.

Phil   Yes.

Cath   Yes!

He stands there, holding the vacuum-cleaner.

Phil   What I said was, we ought to think carefully about it, because it was going to be part of our life. Which it *was*. It *was* part of our life.

Cath   Switch it on, then. Or are we *taking* the dust?

Phil   *Taking* the dust?

Cath   I don't like the dust? What am I trying to say? I used to like the dust. When did I stop liking the dust?

Phil   *I'm* not the one who's changed.

Cath   *The* dust? *Our* dust. Give me that.

She takes the vacuum-cleaner, switches it on and starts to clean the room. She finds the alarm clock on the floor as she works, and shifts it nearer the other remaining items.

Phil   (*shouts over the noise*)   *I'll* do it!

Cath   (*shouts*)   You do the things!

Phil   I said *I'll* do it!

Cath   Do the *things*!

He picks up the remaining items.

Not *that* thing! That's for last!

He dumps an open floppy bag back on the floor. It's exactly where she is going to vacuum.

Not there!

He takes the other things out. She moves the floppy bag in exasperation. It covers up the alarm clock.

No, you *haven't* changed.

He comes back in.

Phil   What?

Cath   You still contradict everything I say.

Phil   *I* contradict?

Cath   I say yes, you say no. I say do, you say don't.

Phil   I say I said yes, you say I said no. I say I'll do that, you say No you won't.

Enter **Pat***, unnoticed in the noise and argument.*

Cath   You wouldn't know what you thought if I didn't say the opposite.

Phil   You wouldn't know what *you* thought if I didn't say something for you to say the opposite to.

Pat *finds the toy dog, and holds it up.*

Cath   I often think you hate me.

Phil   Yes. Sometimes.

Cath *switches off the vacuum-cleaner.*

Cath   You don't!

Phil   You see?

Cath   What?

Phil   Who's contradicting who?

Pat   There's always one thing gets left behind.

Cath   Oh, Pat.

Pat   Don't forget this. You're going to be needing toys now.

She puts the dog down near the floppy bag.

Cath   Oh, Pat! We're going to miss you.

Pat   No, you're not. You'll never think about me again.

Pat *unplugs the vacuum-cleaner and winds up the cord.*

Cath   We will!

Phil   We'll come and see you!

Pat   You won't, you know. You've gone. You've gone. Last you'll see of me – last I'll see of you. And I'll tell you something else, my loves. *I'm* not going to miss *you*. You walk out that door and you've walked off the face of the earth as far as I'm concerned. Who cares? See if *I* mind.

She goes out carrying the vacuum-cleaner, **Phil** *goes to follow her.* **Cath** *stops him.*

Cath   *Do* you?

Phil   What?

Cath   Hate me?

Phil   Oh – no.

Cath   You do.

Phil   And there you go! I say I don't. You say I do.

Cath   You said you did.

Phil   I didn't!

Cath   You did!

Phil   *You* said I did!

Cath   Yes. Well . . .

Phil   Come on.

Cath   All the same, you don't really . . .

Phil   Don't really what? Oh, no!

Cath   No?

Phil   Yes!

Cath   You don't.

Phil   I do! How many times?

Cath   Yes . . .

Phil Yes!

They start to go, then **Cath** *stops and looks round the room. It is completely empty except for the floppy bag.*

Phil *Now* what's the matter?

Cath Nothing. Just . . .

Phil What?

She opens the kitchenette.

Cath That cooker could have done with a bit more work.

He looks into the bathroom.

Phil So could the bath.

Cath Yes. Well . . .

He closes the bathroom.

Phil What are we going to forget?

Cath What do you mean?

Phil Always one thing.

Cath Oh . . .

She looks round, sees the toy dog and picks it up.

Phil Nearly. So, what do you think? Yes or no?

Cath What?

Phil Take it? This place?

Cath Oh . . .

She drops the dog into the floppy bag and looks round.

Yes.

Phil Yes?

Cath Yes!

Phil   Yes.

He opens the door. She stands taking a last look round.

What?

Cath   Oh . . . Nothing. Everything . . .

She quickly goes out. He takes one last look himself.

Phil   We'll never see it again.

He goes out and closes the door behind them. A moment later it opens again, and she runs back in, irritated.

Cath   What are you doing?

She picks up the floppy bag. He reappears in the doorway.

Phil   What am *I* doing?

Cath   You left it there!

Phil   *I* left it there? *We* left it there . . . !

By this time they are outside again, and closing the door. The lights fade, leaving only the alarm clock that was underneath the bag illuminated. It ticks slowly on.

Curtain.

Now You Know

Now You Know was first presented at the Hampstead Theatre, London, on 13 July 1995, with the following cast:

Roy	Paul Gregory
Terry	Adam Faith
Shireen	Luna Rahman
Jacqui	Rosalind Ayres
Liz	Julia Ford
Kevin	Simon Startin
Kent	Dave Fishley
Hilary	Louise Lombard

Directed by Michael Blakemore
Designed by Hayden Griffin
Lighting by Mick Hughes
Sound by John Leonard

Now You Know is adapted from Michael Frayn's novel of the same title, published by Viking (1992) and Penguin (1993).

Act One

The general office of a small political pressure-group.

The accomodation has been improvised out of attics and old storage rooms, high up under the eaves. All the arrangements are cramped and makeshift.

An outer door leads to the staircase down to the street. Beside it is a switchboard/reception desk, closed off by a sliding glass screen. Three inner doors open into a library lined with files, a smaller private office for the campaign director, and a corridor that gives access to the mailroom and to an unseen washroom.

A window opens on to the rooftops outside. A second window in an internal wall gives a little daylight to the otherwise windowless mailroom. This internal window is double-glazed, to soundproof it against the noises of the copier and printer visible inside.

Scene One

Night. **Shireen** *is on the switch. She is in her early twenties, and Asian.* **Kevin** *and* **Kent** *are working inaudibly in the mailroom.* **Kevin** *is thirty, and disabled.* **Kent** *is nineteen, and black.*

At the desk in the general office sits **Jacqui**, *in her forties, trying to work at a VDU. On the other side of the desk perches* **Roy**, *in his mid-thirties, holding a document.* **Terry**, *who is in his late fifties, is walking up and down the room.*

Roy And if you send it to the papers . . .

Terry Disclosing. Right.

Roy Or if you go on one of your television programmes and wave it about in front of the cameras . . .

Terry Knowing or having reasonable cause to believe.

Roy   Knowing or having reasonable cause to believe that it is protected against disclosure . . .

Terry   Only I don't know, do I. I haven't got no reasonable cause.

Roy (*shows document*)   'Home Office. Secret.'

The phone buzzes. **Shireen** *answers it inaudibly.*

Terry   I'm ignorant. I can't read.

Roy   Look, I should be in a meeting. You asked me to come round . . .

Terry   Yes, but someone in the Home Office has leaked this to us. They've leaked it to us because they want us to plaster it all over everything. So how do we do it, Roy?

Roy   I'm giving you my professional opinion.

Terry   I don't want your professional opinion how not to do it. I know how not to do it.

Shireen *slides back her glass screen.*

Shireen   Oh, Terry, it's someone, I couldn't catch his name, he's from the *Telegraph*, it's about the White Paper thing.

Terry (*to* **Shireen**)   We're a campaign for freedom of information, we get our tame brief round, and all he can tell us is how to keep information locked up.

Shireen   Oh, sorry.

Terry *opens the main door, and shows the sign on it saying* OPEN.

Terry (*to* **Roy**)   Why do you think I called this campaign OPEN? Cause that's what we are. Cause any little secrets that go missing can walk in here, have a cup of tea, and then walk out again. (*To* **Shireen**.) What, *Daily Telegraph*? Put him on to Jacqui.

Jacqui Today's the newsletter! I haven't finished the newsletter! Not to mention the membership renewals! .

Terry (*calls*) Liz!

Shireen Only it's getting on for seven.

Roy (*to* **Terry**) I don't know why we don't do this in your office . . .

Liz *comes out of the library. She is in her thirties.*

Terry No secrets here, Roy.

Roy Well, there is, as a matter of fact.

He indicates the document.

Terry Was. Isn't no longer. Not now we got our fingers on it. (*To* **Liz**.) Peter Whatsit, *Telegraph*. White Paper. Tell them.

Liz Tell them what?

Terry Anything they want to know.

Liz *goes back into the library.*

Terry (*calls*) Tell them we got a leak from the Home Office about the Hassam case.

Liz (*puzzled*) Tell the *Telegraph*?

Terry No, Liz. Don't tell no one. Roy here says send them their memo back, don't tell a soul. ·

Shireen I'll put them through . . .

She closes her screen. **Liz** *goes back into the library.*

Roy Look, Terry . . .

He strokes the crown of his head.

Terry Here, put it on.

He feels in a blue cloth bag lying on the desk in front of **Roy**.

Roy What?

Terry   Your hairpiece.

He produces a barrister's wig.

Your brains'll get cold.

Roy   Terry, all I'm saying is this . . .

Terry   I know what you're saying. You're saying
'Official Secrets Act – two years in jail.' You said it
when we done the Ministry of Defence last year. You
said it when we done the Department of Trade and
Industry. Well, don't you two-years me, old son, cause I
know what it means, two years, and it's worse than what
you think.

Roy   I know . . .

Terry   You *don't* know, old lad.

Roy   . . . that you have personal experience . . .

Terry   Right – theft, false pretences, and occasioning
actual bodily harm.

Roy   . . . because it's in our press release. But what
about the others?

Jacqui   Don't worry about me, my loves. Just let me
get on with what I'm doing. And if Terry says do it,
then do it.

Roy   But we have to examine the consequences . . .

Jacqui   No, do it, do it! Tell everyone!

Roy *looks at his watch.*

Roy (*to* **Terry**)   I wish we could talk about this in
private . . .

Jacqui   We'll all go to prison! Wonderful! The whole
staff! At least I shouldn't have to write yet another
appeal for contributions. At least I shouldn't have to
keep on at those boys . . . What *are* they doing?

She bangs on the glass. **Kent** *and* **Kevin** *resume work.*

Roy   Shireen – did she open the envelope? Shireen!

Terry   Don't worry about Shireen.

Shireen *slides her screen back, smiling.*

Shireen   It's nearly seven, Terry. My mum'll kill me.

Roy   Did you open this envelope, Shireen?

Shireen   Yes, well, anything that says just like the name of the campaign.

She takes off her headset and emerges from the switch booth.

Because usually if it's something secret it says kind of 'Terry Little', kind of 'Private and Confidential'.

Roy   But you didn't read it.

Shireen   Well, I saw like 'Home Office', then like 'secret', and I thought, oh hello . . .

Roy   So then you stopped reading.

Shireen   Well, I just read like, you know . . .

Roy   You stopped and you handed it to Terry.

Shireen   Yes, only Terry started jumping up and down and shouting . . .

Roy   Never mind what anybody said. You opened the envelope, you saw the words 'Home Office – secret', and you handed it over. Anyone comes here and asks you questions about it, just tell them that. All right?

Shireen (*smiles*)   All right!

Terry   Don't have to tell Shireen what to say.

Shireen (*laughs*)   Don't worry. Doesn't bother me.

Roy   It might bother you if the police came and asked you questions.

Shireen (*shrugs and smiles*) No, I don't mind. (*Looks at her watch.*) Only Mum's going to be so mad . . .

Terry Get your coat, Shireen.

Shireen I just like sit in there. I've got things to think about. I don't worry about what goes on out here.

She goes out along the corridor.

Roy What about the boys?

He indicates **Kevin** *and* **Kent**, *obliviously idling on the other side of the window.*

Roy Haven't told them anything, have you?

Jacqui What, and stopped them doing my mailout? Look at them.

Kent *picks his nose.*

Terry Kent's busy, anyway.

Jacqui They think we can't see them in there.

Terry With Kevin it's his balls that need scratching . . . There he goes.

Jacqui They think they're invisible, I don't know why.

Terry That's what they all think.

Roy Until we find out what's going on, and you wave it about on television.

Shireen *reappears from the corridor. She stands in front of the window to the mailroom, putting on her coat.*

Shireen Police? It sounds like someone's been murdered or something.

Terry Right. They have.

Roy We don't know.

Shireen Murdered?

She waits, interested.

Roy That's what I'm saying! We still don't know what happened!

Terry Roy, don't give me this legal stuff!

Roy (*picks up document*) All we know from this is that we *don't* know!

Terry We know they was telling us lies!

Roy But we don't know what the truth is!

Terry We know he's dead!

Roy If we'd got the complete story I'd say all right, let's go public, let's take the consequences . . .

Terry We know he was OK when those coppers put him in the patrol van! (*Shows the document.*) We know he wasn't OK when they dragged him out of it!

Kevin *appears from the corridor, followed by* **Kent**.

Kevin (*to* **Terry**) Three minutes past . . . Three minutes past . . .

Terry Three minutes past seven. I know. Off you go, then, you two.

Shireen This is Mr Hassam?

Terry Oh, now we've got her interested.

Kevin *makes his way towards the door, followed by* **Kent**, *but is distracted by the letter on the desk in front of* **Roy**.

Kevin (*looking at document*) I don't understand . . .

Terry And we know that three hours later they look in his cell and he's mysteriously suffering from a slight case of death.

Roy Which may have been the result of a heart-attack.

Terry   Right, or the first symptom of a cold coming on.

Kevin   I don't . . .

Kent (*to* **Kevin**)   Come on! They don't want you nosing around.

Kevin   I don't understand . . .

Terry *takes the document out of* **Kevin**'s *hands.*

Terry   Only now for some reason we got the riot shields out, we got petrol bombs flying all over the West Midlands, we got questions in the House – and we got *this.*

Kevin   . . . the logical force of their argument.

Terry   No, right, *I* don't understand the logical force of their argument, neither, Kevin. But then I don't understand the logical force of beating yourself to death. I don't understand the logical force of stopping you and me knowing about it. I don't understand the logical force of letting the buggers get away with it.

Liz *appears in the doorway of the library.*

Roy   Liz? What do *you* think?

Jacqui   My God, we're not going to start *voting* on it, are we?

Liz (*smiles*)   Why not?

Jacqui   Why not? Because we don't work like that, my pet!

Liz (*smiles*)   Don't we?

Jacqui   We never *have*, my sweet! We've never had debates, we've never taken votes.

Liz   Perhaps we should have done.

Jacqui   There's something absolutely subversive about

you, Liz, my precious.

Liz I thought there was supposed to be something subversive about all of us.

Jacqui What do you mean?

Liz Nothing. What about Shireen? What does she think?

Shireen Oh, I don't mind! It doesn't worry me!

Jacqui (*to* **Liz**) You sit out there grinning away with your hair in your eyes. No one knows *what* you're up to.

Terry (*to* **Jacqui**) Come on, love, don't start on Liz.

Liz What about the boys, then? What do they think?

Kevin You can trust me . . .

Terry We know that, Kev.

Kevin You can trust me . . .

Liz How about Kent?

Kent What?

Terry Instant look of being somewhere else, with witnesses to prove it.

Roy What do you think, Kent?

Terry I'll tell you what Kent thinks. Don't know. That's what Kent thinks.

Roy Kent?

Kent (*shrugs*) Don't know.

Terry Don't know, right. That's two in favour, two against, two don't knows . . .

Kevin You can trust me . . .

Terry Three in favour. Right.

Jacqui Stop! Stop! Stop all this! Look, my loves, I

didn't drop everything and throw in my lot with Terry because I wanted to hold *debates.* I did it because I believed in him, and whatever he thought I thought – because I was ready to follow him to the ends of the earth!

Hilary *enters unnoticed through the open door from the stairs. She is a quiet, serious woman of about thirty. She stops in the doorway at the sight of them all.*

Roy (*gets to his feet*)   Yes, well, if this is some kind of religious order . . .

Jacqui   All right! Why not?

Roy   And our friend here is some kind of Messiah . . .

Jacqui   At least we might get something decided, something done, something improved in the world!

They become aware of **Hilary**'s *presence.*

Hilary   I'm sorry . . .

Terry   Come in.

Hilary   I'll wait outside.

Terry   Wait inside. (*Shows the sign on the door.*) OPEN, look. Open by name, open by nature. Who do you want?

Hilary   It doesn't matter.

She begins to go out again.

Terry   Come back!

Hilary   You're obviously busy . . .

Terry   Yes, so come and help us. Close the door . . . (*To* **Roy**.) Member of the public, right?

Roy (*stroking his head awkwardly*)   Terry . . .

Terry   Come in off the street. Never seen her before. Just the job. (*To* **Hilary**.) Know about Mr Hassam, do you, darling?

Hilary *looks quickly at* **Roy**, *then back at* **Terry**.

Hilary (*guarded*)   Mr Hassam?

Roy   Hold on, Terry . . .

Terry   The one who's on TV. The one who's in all the papers.

Hilary   Yes?

Terry   Read this, then, my love. This is what you *don't* know about Mr Hassam.

He hands her the document.

(*To* **Roy**.) Decision. Right? End of argument. I've done it. I've disclosed. Ring Special Branch.

Roy   Yes. Well . . .

Hilary (*to* **Roy**, *not looking at the document*)   I'm sorry. I waited. But . . .

Roy   I know. I'm sorry. I was just coming. I didn't realise this thing was going to go on.

He takes the document out of her hands, and holds it out to **Terry**.

Terry   Oh, I see! This is her! (*To* **Hilary**.) You're the meeting. He kept saying, 'I'm supposed to be in a meeting.'

He takes the document.

Roy   Yes, well, we must be on our way.

Terry   So at last we've met the famous lady-friend. Lovely.

He takes her hand.

Heard all about you. Haven't we, Jacqui? Always going on about you, he is. One moment you're in Chambers together – next thing we know you're living together.

Hilary *glances at* **Roy**.

Roy　Terry...

Terry　Two barristers in one bed! God help us! So – who's prosecuting, who's defending?

Roy　Terry...

Terry　Right, don't answer that. Just say hello to Jacqui before you go, since she's the one who keeps us all solvent, God knows how.

Jacqui　Hello.

Terry (*to* **Hilary**)　And this is Liz, before she melts away like an ice-cream in front of your eyes.

Liz　Yes, we have actually...

She melts back into the library, embarrassed.

Terry　Oh, you have. Lovely.

Kent *edges out of the main door.*

Terry　And that's Kent, that was. What's he doing? Nothing. Where's he going?

Kent　Nowhere.

Terry　Nowhere. Go on, then, Kent.

Kent *goes*.

Roy　Anyway...

Terry　And Shireen on the switch. Hear that smile of hers down the other end of the line.

Shireen (*smiles*)　Hello.

Terry (*to* **Shireen**)　Don't keep your mum waiting, then.

Shireen　No, but I don't know why everyone's so

excited about this Mr Hassam person. No one got excited when my friend's uncle was murdered. No one did anything when my sister's boyfriend got beaten up. It's just like . . . funny.

Shireen *goes out.*

Terry Very funny. Must be. She's still smiling about it.

Kevin You can trust me . . .

Jacqui And Kevin.

Terry What can we say about you, Kev?

Kevin You can trust me . . .

Terry Right. You can trust him. Off you go, then, Kevin.

Kevin *indicates the document.*

Kevin . . . not to be garrulous.

Terry That's a lovely thought, Kevin.

Kevin *goes out.*

Terry It takes him a long time to get off the ground, old Kev. But once he's up in the air . . . up in the air he is, good and proper. That's us, then. Off you go. Come and see us again. Oh – me. I'm Terry.

Hilary I know.

Terry (*to* **Roy**) She knew. Seen me on the box.

Hilary No, it was at a party.

Terry Once seen never forgotten.

Hilary No.

Roy So, if I could just have my wig . . .

Terry (*to* **Hilary**) You got one of these, have you?

He puts it on her.

Hilary (*takes it off*)   No.

Terry   No? No tea-cosy?

Hilary   I'm not a barrister.

Terry (*baffled*)   Not a barrister?

Hilary *looks at* **Roy**.

Roy   This isn't Fenella. I don't know why you assume it's Fenella. This is Hilary.

Terry   Oh. Sorry about that. Hilary?

Hilary   Yes.

Roy   I did try to tell you.

Terry   Hilary. Right. (*To* **Roy**.) So you and Fenella . . . ?

Roy   We're fine. Only Fenella's in Bristol. She's doing a public inquiry.

Terry   Oh. Right.

Roy   Hilary and I arranged to meet for a drink.

Terry   Oh, lovely.

Roy   For heaven's sake.

Terry   I need one of these things and all.

He takes the wig back and puts it on back to front, so that it covers his eyes.

Roy   And if I could just have that . . .

Terry *gives him the wig.*

Terry   Sorry, Roy. Nice to meet you, Hilary. No, you're not a barrister. One look at you and I know that.

Ushers them to the door.

So what are you, then, Hilary?

Hilary   I'm a civil servant.

Terry *laughs*.

Terry   Right! You're a civil servant!

Roy (*to* **Hilary**)   Come on . . .

Hilary   I know what you think of civil servants.

Terry   No – laughing at him, not you. Consorting
with the enemy!

Hilary   That's what I mean.

Terry   Only joking, Hilary. I've nothing against civil
servants, believe me. All in favour of them. Just want to
see a bit more of you all.

Roy (*to* **Terry**, *holding the door open for* **Hilary**)   I'll bring
my draft of the report in next week . . .

Hilary (*to* **Terry**)   Why?

Terry   Why what?

Hilary   Why do you want to see a bit more of us all?

Roy   Oh, for heaven's sake . . .

Terry   No, I'll tell you. Because you're a bashful lot,
Hilary. You done an awful lot of messing around in my
life, and I never had a chance to talk to you about it.

Hilary   Go on, then.

Terry   What, and talk to you about it?

Hilary   Yes. What have we done?

Roy (*to* **Hilary**)   We are a little pushed for time . . .

Terry (*to* **Hilary**)   Well, first off, Hilary, my love, you
nicked me for something I never done.

Roy   Oh dear.

Jacqui (*to* **Hilary**)   This is when he was a child! (*To* **Terry**.) She wasn't even born, my sweet.

Terry   The people you work with, Hilary. Your mates.

Roy   Look, let's get one thing straight.

He closes the door.

It doesn't help our cause in any way to be rude and aggressive to public servants in private . . .

Liz *appears in the doorway of the library.*

Hilary   No, I asked.

Terry   Yes, she don't need you defending her, Roy. She can look after herself. Can't you, Hilary? She's just as clever as what you are, I know that, or she wouldn't have passed the exam. Sit down, Hilary.

Roy   Terry, please!

Terry (*to* **Hilary**)   Sit down.

Jacqui   Terry, they've got to go!

Terry   Sit down.

Hilary *sits down.*

Terry (*without looking round*)   And you, Liz. You're on the jury.

Liz *vanishes back into the library.*

Roy   Look . . .

Terry *sits down opposite* **Hilary**.

Terry (*looking at* **Hilary**)   I am looking. You look, too. You might learn something. (*To* **Hilary**) Yes, and when my mum died you shipped me and my brothers off to homes. One of us this way, one of us that. I ended up in Staffordshire. Why can't I be with my brothers? Because. Never you mind. You just do as you're told. Two years I was in that place, Hilary, and you never told me why.

Roy   No, well, since this all happened forty or fifty years ago . . .

Terry   Yes, all you done since *you* been around is listen in to my phone calls and steam open my letters.

Roy   No one's listened in to your phone calls! No one's steamed open your letters!

Jacqui (*to* **Hilary**)   Anyway, I don't suppose he means you personally.

Terry   No, I'm not being *personal*. *I'm* not being personal, *you're* not being personal. Never anything personal. Not your department, the nosepokers, I know that. You're not in the Home Office. You're in the bit that helps old ladies across the road.

Hilary *gazes at him. He gazes back.* **Liz** *reappears in the doorway to the library.*

Roy   Right, you've made your point . . .

Terry   Bet your mum and dad are proud of you, Hilary. Nice people, are they? Nice little house, nice little garden? Not one of the nobs, are you, like old Roy. Didn't come all that easy for you, any more than what it did for me. Went down the road to school every day, did you, Hilary? Never messed around with boys? Did all your homework? Passed all your exams? Went off to college? Phoned home every Sunday? Mum and Dad come up to see you get your degree?

She is still staring at him. He is gazing back at her.

Roy (*to* **Hilary**)   You don't *have* to sit here and listen politely.

Terry   No, *has* to be civil, don't you, Hilary, if you're a civil servant. One more question, then, and I won't say another word.

He shows her the document.

That poor Mr Hassam the Home Office have been looking after. How did he manage to beat himself to death without anyone even noticing he was doing it?

Roy (*decisively*)   Come on.

He goes to the door. **Hilary** *remains sitting, looking at* **Terry**.

Terry   What – no comment? Very sensible. Know things I don't know. Lot you could say if only you chose, etcetera. Not your policy to comment on allegations of this nature.

She continues to look at him. He looks levelly back. **Liz** *vanishes again.*

Roy   Hilary . . .

Terry   A cat may look at a king.

Jacqui   Only which of you is the cat and which of you is the king?

Hilary *looks away. She gets up.*

Hilary   I never had a father. I was brought up by my mother, and we didn't have a house, and we didn't have a garden.

Pause.

Terry   OK, Hilary. Fair enough. A very frank answer, even if it's not the answer to the question I asked. Lot franker and more informative than what you usually get from a Government department.

He puts his hand on her arm.

I never had much of a father, me neither. He buggered off and left us when I was two.

Roy   Anyway, I've given you my opinion. I imagine you'll do what you usually do, which is what you were going to do anyway. And I'll bring that report in.

Terry   What report?

Roy   Secrecy in the legal profession.

Terry   Oh, right.

Roy *and* **Hilary** *go out.*

Terry   Walked right into that one.

Jacqui   I knew it wasn't Fenella.

Terry (*laughs*)   He'll be the worst of the lot, old Roy, when they make him a minister. Secrets? He'll be taking the name off the front of the Ministry.

Jacqui   He's only behaving the way most men do, my love.

Terry   You got to laugh, though.

Jacqui   Have you?

Terry   What – me?

Jacqui   I'm not saying anything.

Terry   When have I ever?

Jacqui   Never. Never.

Liz *appears in the doorway, putting on her coat.*

Terry   What – last summer?

Jacqui   I haven't said a word.

Terry   I know what you thought, but it wasn't so.

Jacqui   No.

Liz   Sorry.

She goes back into the library.

Terry   Come on, Liz, if you're coming!

Liz *reappears uncertainly.*

Liz   No, I'd forgotten something . . .

Terry   You don't have to keep bolting back into your hole, my love, like some little furry animal. We're talking about that girl that come to do work experience last summer, only it's not so, it's not so.

Liz *goes to the main door, smiling.*

Terry   So that was another of your strange chums.

Liz   Well, I met her once.

Terry   Never said, though, did you?

Liz   No ... well ...

Terry   Just went back into your hole and left us all to fall on our faces.

Liz   It was a bit ...

Terry   Awkward.

Liz   Yes.

Terry   Same as you.

Liz *smiles.*

Terry   Another smiler. You and Shireen. Funny lot, smilers. Never know what's going on round the back.

Liz (*smiles*)   See you in the morning.

She departs.

Terry   Her. Shireen. The boys. You. Five little worlds we got in here. And all of them a bit of a mystery, when you come right down to it.

Jacqui   Six.

Terry   Six?

Jacqui   Yourself.

Terry   No mystery about me, my love. Anyway, what's wrong with a bit of mystery? Moderation in all things.

He looks at the document.

But I give her the memo! I give it straight back to the Civil Service, just like Roy said!

Jacqui   So what are you going to do with it?

Terry   Put it away.

He puts it on the desk.

Think about it. Maybe they'll send us some more. Don't add up to much on its own.

Jacqui   That's not what you told Roy.

Terry   No, well, I come on a bit strong. *You* come on a bit strong, and all.

Jacqui   Did I?

He stands behind her as she works, and massages her neck.

Terry   Give it a rest, love. After seven.

Jacqui   There's still the accounts . . .

Terry   Tell you what, missis. I'll take you out and buy you dinner. Once-off, *ex gratia*, no precedents established.

Jacqui   It's Tuesday. It's my mother.

Terry   Oh, right.

He stops massaging her neck, and takes off his jacket.

Jacqui   No reason why you shouldn't come with me, though, darling.

Terry   Fellow got up at the Tory Party Conference couple of years ago, remember?

He carries the jacket into his private office, and reappears, taking off his tie.

Described me as a dangerous extremist. Not so, my love. Only thing I'm extreme about is moderation.

Jacqui   You could just come for half-an-hour.

Terry   Moderation. OK?

He goes back into his office. **Jacqui** *begins to fold up her files.*

Jacqui   You are coming home on Friday, though?

Terry *reappears with a clean shirt on a wire hanger. He hangs it up and takes off the shirt he is wearing.*

Terry   Friday?

Jacqui   It's Poops's half-term. I did tell you.

Terry   Oh, right . . . Roy's little mystery, though. If someone said what was she like I'd say a helping of rather brainy mashed potatoes. I mean, all there on the plate in front of you. No surprises. Always the same with these mysteries, isn't it. When you finally get to meet them there's no mystery about them.

Jacqui   You know Poops is riding Pippy at the local hunt thing on Saturday.

Terry   Your ex'll be there.

Jacqui   I mean I'll be out all day – you can take Bicky and Scrumps for a walk.

Jacqui *takes the dirty shirt into his office.*

Terry   You got your own life out there, though, haven't you. You got your house, you got your friends. You got Poops and Pippy. You got the dogs.

Jacqui *emerges from his office, holding socks and underwear.*

Jacqui   In the filing cabinet . . .

She sniffs at them.

All mixed up with the clean.

Terry   You got the cat. Got me, come to that. Saturdays and Sundays.

Jacqui   Why don't you *give* it to me?

She puts all the underwear into a bag.

And that sleeping-bag must be absolutely crawling by now . . .

Terry   No, but that'd be extremism.

Jacqui   Being there in the week?

Terry   Living out there. For me. The middle of things, that's my territory, my love. Down Westminster, up Soho, meet a few people, find out what's going on. Half a mile this way, half a mile that way. Moderation.

Jacqui   I meant what I said, though.

Terry   What, believing in me?

Jacqui   That hasn't changed, my sweet.

Terry   Ends of the earth?

Jacqui   Of which this office is one, as far as I'm concerned. I wish you'd let me take that sleeping-bag.

Terry   Saving it up for Christmas.

He gives her a kiss.

Jacqui   I'll give your love to my mother.

Terry   Night, then.

Jacqui   Night.

Terry   Know where I'm going tonight?

Jacqui   No. And don't want to.

She departs. He kicks off his shoes.

Terry   Right, then, white tie and tails.

He takes his trousers off, then notices the uncurtained window. He calls out into the night.

Keep looking, darling, there's no charge . . . Open to the

public twenty-four hours a day, that's us.

He folds the trousers, and continues to talk to the outside world, or to himself.

Anything you want to know, just ask . . . Is it me? Yes, it is. See someone and it looks like me – it's me, put money on it. Any more questions . . . ? Go on, then . . . What's my greatest satisfaction in life? – The Campaign. Being Director of the Campaign – What's my greatest regret? – No kids. All right?

He takes the trousers into his office, then puts his head back.

Open book, that's me.

He goes into the office, and emerges with a dark suit. He holds it up and inspects it as he talks.

Put it another way – I got my story ready. That's from when I was so high. Walking down the street, feeling the handle on the odd car, just in case. Up zooms the law. 'What are you up to, son . . . ?'

He fetches a clothes brush from his office and brushes the suit.

No good saying 'Nothing', like old Kent, cause then it's: 'Right, loitering with intent – you're nicked.' So let's try this one: 'Going down the Council offices, my dad works there.' Might be true, all they know – might be trouble. And sometimes . . .

He hangs up the suit.

. . . off they zoom again.

He goes out into the corridor. The sound of taps being turned on. **Hilary** *comes in through the main door. She looks round uncertainly.* **Terry**, *off, splashes water over his head, snorts, and gasps with satisfaction.* **Hilary** *frowns, and decides to wait.* **Terry** *comes back in, still in his underwear, vigorously towelling his face and head.*

Terry (*under the towel*) I haven't got many qualifications

for running a political campaign. I'm an ignorant
bastard. But I got one: I'm me, and everyone knows it.
Anyone wants me they can usually find me.

He takes the towel away from his face.

Hilary I'm sorry. I thought you were talking to
someone . . . I thought Roy might be . . . We had a
slight disagreement. I thought he might have . . .
Anyway . . .

She opens the door to go.

Terry Sit down! Five minutes, he'll suss you're here.

Hilary Tell him I've gone home, will you, if he comes
back?

Terry Or come out and have supper with me.

Hilary No, thank you.

Terry Suit yourself.

*He puts on the clean shirt and hangs up the hanger. She stands in
the doorway looking at him.*

What? Knees? Nice, aren't they?

Hilary It was a charity evening.

Terry What was a charity evening?

Hilary Where I saw you before. You were talking to
a woman who happened to be a doctor.

Terry Was I?

Hilary You were telling her why you hated the
medical profession.

Terry Good memory you got, Hilary.

Hilary I watched you. I watched you quite carefully. I
watched her, too.

Terry Why, what was she doing?

Hilary   She was putting her head on one side, and making a funny little face, and laughing.

Terry   You're not laughing.

Hilary   No.

She looks round the room.

Terry   What – comic way to live? I'll tell you something, Hilary . . . Only I'll put my trousers on first. I don't know why, but I can't hold forth in my underpants.

He puts on his trousers.

Right, so listen, Hilary – and it's taken me half-a-century to find this out: everyone lives in a comic way. Everyone? *Everyone.* They all got some funny arrangement in their lives, they all got some special little way they're allowed to be different from everybody else, only no one but them knows about it. The people you work with, Hilary – they look normal? They come in on the train every day, they got a wife and kids? Watch out, sweetheart, because that means they got something going on somewhere that's a whole lot more comic than what this is.

She sits down in **Jacqui***'s chair. He sits opposite her, and gazes at her.*

Hilary   Look . . .

Terry   I'm looking.

Hilary   Yes, and that's another of your little tricks.

Terry   What?

Hilary   This.

Terry   See into your soul, Hilary.

Hilary *looks away.*

Terry   Funny, isn't it – nobody wants their soul seeing into.

Hilary I've seen you on the television, too. I've heard
you on the radio. You don't argue, you don't present a
case – you simply put on a performance. You make it
sound as if you're just being the plain reasonable man.
But you're not – you're being completely unreasonable.
You say a lot of funny things, but you're not funny,
you're very aggressive, and very destructive. It makes me
angry. I'm sorry to be so un-Civil-Service-like.

Terry *picks up the kettle.*

Terry So, what, cup of tea?

Hilary Yes, and that's typical of the way you argue!

Terry I'm not arguing, Hilary. I'm listening.

Pause.

Also waiting.

He offers the kettle. She ignores it.

Hilary Look . . .

Terry Got it from Roy, didn't you. All this 'Look'.
Then he has a feel round the back of his head, see
whether he's got his rug on . . . OK. No more
interruptions, no answering back, no tea.

He puts the kettle down.

Hilary It's the same for us as for everybody else. We
all have to be free to discuss things frankly in private.
To say what we truly think without hurting people's
feelings or destroying their reputations. To disagree with
each other in private, and then to present a common
front in public. I don't agree with all our decisions, of
course I don't, and it would be ridiculous if I couldn't
say so while they're being made. But it would be just as
ridiculous if I then went round telling everyone I didn't
agree with what we'd decided.

Pause.

And even if you *did* manage to find out what went on you'd discover most of it was so dull you wouldn't be interested.

She picks up the document.

And when something goes wrong then we've got to have some privacy while we investigate, otherwise we'll never find out what happened. We've also got to avoid saying anything that might make the situation worse.

Terry   Biscuit?

He offers her a packet. She takes no notice of it.

Hilary   As a matter of fact it's not very easy work. And you're right, some of it's quite distasteful. So's what dustmen do, and sewage workers. And yes, it's horrible not being able to talk to people about what you're doing. I suppose you're thinking, Then why am I having a relationship with someone in your campaign? Well, I'm *not* having a relationship with him.

Terry *offers the biscuits again.*

Terry   Special slimming ones. Made of sawdust.

Hilary   I don't even understand what that's supposed to mean – a relationship.

Terry   Jacqui gets them from the health place.

Hilary   He's just someone I happen to know.

He takes one himself and puts the packet down.

Terry   So how long's this been going on, Hilary, this non-relationship?

Hilary   I don't want to talk about it.

Terry   Fair enough. Not another word.

He sits down at the desk opposite her. She abstractedly takes a wafer from the packet, breaks it in half, but doesn't eat it.

Hilary And yes, I *did* work hard at school, if you
want to know. And things *weren't* easy – they were
extremely difficult, because I had to do a job in the
evenings, and another one at the weekends. And yes, I
got a first, and yes, my mother's proud of me, and no,
I'm not ashamed of it.

She puts the two halves of the wafer down on the desk.

Terry Ever wonder about your dad, Hilary?

She takes another wafer out of the packet.

Sorry. Another question. Slipped out.

Hilary I don't want to talk about that, either. I
shouldn't have said anything about it.

She breaks the wafer in half.

Anyway, I don't know anything about him. I don't know
what his job was. I don't even know his name. My
mother never talked about him. We didn't talk about
things like that.

She breaks the halves up into little pieces.

Terry Nevada.

Hilary Sorry?

Terry What you put me in mind of. All very nice and
quiet, but then underground there's a nuclear test going
on.

She drops the pieces on the desk and takes another wafer.

Hilary There was a lot that Mum and I never talked
about, now I come to think of it. I suppose it was good
training for my work.

She smiles bleakly.

Terry Oh, nice.

Hilary What?

Terry You smiled. Lovely. You're a lovely girl, Hilary.

Hilary I must go.

She remains.

Terry I'll tell you a funny thing, Hilary. Your mum's not the only one who's proud of you. *I'm* proud of you. All right, I come on a bit strong before. Always coming on a bit strong. So people tell me. Jealous, who knows? No clever kids of my own, you see, Hilary. No kids at all. And I wasn't very nice to my mum. Me and my brothers used to give her hell, she didn't know whether she was coming or going, I think it was us that killed her. So I'm very glad you was good to yours, and you worked hard, and you did well. You're a good person, Hilary.

He wipes his eyes.

Don't worry. Don't mean all that much – it don't take a great deal to make me cry . . . Only it makes me think the Civil Service can't be so bad after all if it's got people like you working for it . . . Anyway, here's what *I'm* after in life, Hilary: heaven. You know what it says about heaven in the Bible – it's built of gold. You know that – everyone knows that. But what sort of gold? You don't know, Hilary, do you. I'll tell you: gold like unto clear glass. That's the bit they all forget. Gold like unto clear glass. Transparent gold. All the walls of all the houses in heaven. A golden light in all the rooms. Nothing hidden. Everything visible. All kinds of comic arrangements you can see inside those rooms, Hilary. People living in their offices, with their suits on coathooks and their clean shirts in the stationery cupboard.

The switchboard buzzer begins to buzz softly.

People living half the week with their sister-in-law, and

half the week with the postman's grandmother.

She looks at the switch. He gets up and crosses to it.

But all of it open for the world to see. So no one thinks there's anything comic about it.

*He takes out **Shireen***'s *headset.*

And if that's the way it's going to be in heaven, why wait? Why not try and make it like that here on earth? (*Into headset.*) Hello ... ?

She watches him.

Oh, hello, Roy ... Has she come back here ... ?

He turns to look at her. She looks away, and resumes breaking the wafers up.

No − why'd she come back here ... ? Talking to myself. Who'd you think I was talking to ... ? OK, Roy, any sign of her, I'll tell her ...

*He repeats to **Hilary** what **Roy** is saying.*

You've gone home, you'll ring her in the morning ... Right ...

He puts the headset back, and crosses back to her. He stands looking down at her.

Awful mess you're making with them biscuits, Hilary.

Hilary   Yes.

She stops, and dusts the crumbs off her fingers. He holds out his hands.

What?

Terry   Coat.

She stands up and unbuttons her overcoat.

Slow, aren't I? Got its advantages, though.

He puts her overcoat aside. She leans back against the desk, watching his hands as he begins to unbutton her shirt.

Everybody else in the world knows the answer to everything already – they always did – it's no surprise to them. Suddenly I tumble it as well – and it really hits me.

He stops, looks at the uncurtained window, then crosses to the light-switches.

OK – we haven't got to heaven yet.

He turns out the main lights. Only a shaded desk-light remains.

I'll tell you what I like about women, Hilary . . .

He resumes unbuttoning her shirt.

. . . you never know what they're up to.

He unbuttons his own shirt.

And I'll tell you what women like about me: they always do.

She turns out the desk light. Blackout.

Scene Two

Day. **Shireen** *is on the switch,* **Kevin** *and* **Kent** *are in the mailroom,* **Kevin** *working,* **Kent** *gazing into space and picking his nose. Enter* **Jacqui** *through the main door, in her overcoat.*

Jacqui   *Thirteen* separate beggars between Waterloo and here this morning, which I think may be a record.

Liz *looks out of the library. It's probably* **Liz** *that* **Jacqui** *is addressing.*

Jacqui   The 8.18 was cancelled . . . Hello, my sweet.

Liz *smiles vaguely.*

Jacqui   All right, my pet?

Liz Fine.

She goes back into the library.

Jacqui *Plus* a signals failure at Staines . . .

Shireen *slides back the screen on the switch.*

Shireen Oh, Jacqui, someone called for Terry, I think
it was Steve something. And those people in
Birmingham, they said you'd know what it was about.

She hands over the morning post.

Terry's out having a bath.

Jacqui Oh, thank you, my pet. Wonderful. Lovely.
And the doorway downstairs, my precious . . .

Shireen Oh, the doorway!

Jacqui Knee-deep in cardboard boxes again.

Shireen Sorry, Jacqui, I forgot.

Jacqui It's not that I *mind* those two girls sleeping in
the doorway. There but for the grace of God. What I
cannot see for the life of me, though, is why it should
be muggins here who has to fold up their boxes for
them *every* morning.

Shireen I'll do it tomorrow, Jacqui.

Shireen *closes her screen.*

Jacqui And who Steve something is, and what all this
is about people in Birmingham, I have naturally not the
faintest notion.

She bangs on the window of the mailroom. **Kevin** *and* **Kent**
look at her.

Jacqui Yes, I'm here! Yes, I'm smiling at you! Yes,
I'm going to go on smiling at you! Smile, smile, smile!

Reluctantly **Kent** *begins to work.* **Jacqui** *sits down at her desk,
still watching* **Kent**.

Jacqui   And Kevin, of course, will shortly be retiring to the loo for half the morning . . . It's like Poops getting Pippy started when he's in one of his bloody-minded moods – sheer heels and willpower . . .

Liz *comes in from the library.*

Liz   So what was decided?

Jacqui   What about, my love?

Liz   Our leak.

She picks up the document from **Jacqui***'s desk.*

Jacqui   Oh, no! He didn't leave it lying on the desk?

She takes it back.

This is supposed to be secret! I know we're against it, but honestly!

Liz   What are we doing with it, though?

Jacqui *is examining the document with distaste.*

Jacqui   Sitting on it, apparently. Rolling about on it. Look – it's all *crumpled*! What's been happening in here! Shireen! Shireen, my precious!

Shireen *slides the screen back.*

Jacqui   Who's been at my desk? Look, everything – it's *all* crumpled!

Shireen   Oh, no!

She emerges from the switch.

Jacqui   The pencils – they're all everywhere . . . ! That's not where the stapler lives . . . Where's my address-book . . . ? Someone's been . . . *crashing about* all over the top of my desk . . . !

Shireen   Oh, Jacqui!

Jacqui   And my slimbreads! There's only one left!

Someone's eaten them!

Shireen Oh, no, not your slimbreads!

Liz No one *ever* eats your slimbreads.

Jacqui As it happens I haven't had any breakfast this morning . . .

Shireen Oh, Jacqui, I'll run out and get you some more!

Jacqui No, but it's the *principle* of the thing. I'm perfectly happy to share. All people have got to do is come and *ask* me.

She stops. She has found broken pieces of slimming wafer among the files on her desk.

Liz What?

Shireen All like little broken pieces! They've like . . . snapped them all in half!

Jacqui This isn't even thoughtlessness. This is wanton destruction.

Shireen Oh, Jacqui, isn't that awful!

Liz *laughs.*

Jacqui Yes, well, it may amuse you. But this I am not standing for.

Shireen Perhaps the boys . . .

They turn to look at **Kent** *and* **Kevin***, who are watching them through the glass.*

Liz Oh, I don't think so. Not your slimbreads.

Kent *and* **Kevin** *go back to work.* **Jacqui** *starts towards the corridor, still holding the empty packet.*

Liz No, Jacqui! Please! Don't start on the boys . . . !

Jacqui And of course at once you take their side!

She goes out.

Liz I can't bear it when she's like this . . .

Jacqui *appears in the mailroom. Inaudibly she gestures at* **Kent** *and* **Kevin** *with the slimbread packet.* **Shireen** *gazes at the scene, absorbed.* **Liz** *looks, then looks away, not knowing what to do.*

Shireen My sister keeps going on at me. 'You've got to get off that switch, Shireen!' she says, 'you've got to do audio!' 'Oh,' I go, 'I quite like being on the switch.' 'Don't be silly, Shireen!' she goes. 'You *don't* like it! It's boring, nothing ever happens!'

Kevin *is clutching an old ex-army haversack to himself, shaking his head.*

Liz Oh, no, not his bag!

Shireen What's he got in that bag, anyway?

Liz I can't watch this!

She goes agitatedly to the door of the library.

Shireen She's really going for him.

Liz She *knows* he never lets anyone see in that bag! I don't know how you can stand there and watch!

Liz *takes refuge in the library.*

Shireen (*absorbed*) It's like, you know, this person's being tortured, only you've got the sound turned down . . .

Hilary *enters through the main door, and stops. She is carrying a bulky brown envelope.*

Hilary Oh . . .

She stops uncertainly.

Shireen (*smiles*) Oh, hello!

Hilary *hesitates.*

Shireen Come in! We're having all like dramas this morning. Jacqui's on the warpath!

Hilary I was just...

She looks round the room.

Shireen He's not here. Roy? He's in court this morning.

Liz *appears in the library doorway to see what's going on. The confrontation between* **Jacqui** *and* **Kevin** *has subsided into more general nagging.*

Hilary No...

Shireen Oh, what – Terry?

Liz You want Terry?

Shireen He's just out having a bath.

Liz Hello...

Hilary Hello.

Shireen Sit down!

Hilary No, well, I was only going to...

She looks uncertainly at the envelope.

Shireen I'll give it to him.

She takes it.

Oh – it's a Private and Confidential. Lovely. He always likes getting Private and Confidentials! And lots in it, too!

She puts it on the counter of the switch.

I'll put it over there, look, with his other ones.

Liz This is for Terry?

She picks up the envelope and looks at it, puzzled.

Shireen He'll be like a kid with a birthday present,

won't he, Liz.

Hilary It's not anything very interesting. It's just ...
well ... bits and pieces ...

Shireen Oh, don't tell us, don't tell us! We're not
supposed to know!

The phone buzzes. **Shireen** *goes back into the switch and puts
her headset back on.*

(*To* **Hilary**.) Only watch out for Jacqui! Someone's
messed up her desk – they've broken up all her like slim
things! (*Into headset.*) Hello, OPEN ...

She closes the screen. **Hilary** *looks at the desk.* **Liz** *sees her
look.* **Hilary** *looks away.* **Liz** *looks at the desk, then at*
Hilary, *then at the envelope, then at* **Hilary** *again.*

Liz It wasn't you that ... ?

Hilary What?

Liz Her desk.

Hilary *looks at the desk, then looks away.*

Hilary I've got to go.

Liz I didn't mean that. I just meant ...

Hilary Could I have it?

She holds out her hand for the envelope.

Liz This? I thought ... ?

Hilary I've changed my mind.

Pause.

Liz Yes. All right.

She hands **Hilary** *the envelope.* **Jacqui** *enters.*

Jacqui He's got *something* hidden in that bag, I know
that. And the *smell* in there ...

She stops at the sight of **Hilary**.

Jacqui (*coldly*)   Roy? He's not here. He's never here in the day.

Hilary   No ... no ...

Liz   She's just going.

Jacqui   He's in court. I imagine.

Hilary   Yes, I think he is.

Liz   She's just going!

Jacqui *sees the envelope that* **Hilary** *is holding.*

Jacqui   What's this?

Liz   Oh ...

Jacqui   For us?

Liz   No. Well ...

Jacqui (*takes it and looks at it*)   For Terry ... For *Terry*?

She looks at **Hilary**.

Hilary   It was just something ... It doesn't matter ...

She tries to take the envelope from **Jacqui**.

Jacqui   Wait a moment. 'Private and Confidential'? For Terry?

She looks at **Hilary**. **Liz** *looks anxiously from one to the other.*

Hilary   Yes.

Jacqui   Oh. *Oh.*

Hilary   I'll bring it back another time.

She hold out her hand for the envelope. **Jacqui**'s *manner changes.*

Jacqui   Sit down, my sweet.

Hilary   I made a mistake ...

Jacqui   I'm not going to open it.

Hilary   I want to just check . . .

Jacqui   Sit down.

Hilary   I think I may have put something in I didn't mean to . . .

Jacqui   We can all have a cup of coffee together while we wait for Terry.

She fetches the kettle.

Hilary   Thank you, but I can't really . . .

Jacqui *draws out a chair for* **Hilary** *and waits.*

Liz (*to* **Jacqui**)   I think if she wants it back . . .

Jacqui *hands* **Liz** *the kettle.*

Jacqui (*to* **Liz**)   Just fill this, will you, my love?

Liz *stands holding the kettle.* **Jacqui** *indicates the chair to* **Hilary**.

Jacqui   Here!

Hilary   Well . . .

She sits reluctantly.

Jacqui   My desk. The nerve-centre of the entire operation! No, but in fact it *is*, because Terry's always at work on it as well . . . (*To* **Liz**.) Kettle!

Liz *remains.*

Jacqui (*to* **Hilary**)   I'd offer you one of my slimbreads, but someone – no one here, of course, oh no – some mysterious intruder – I haven't got to the bottom of this yet . . .

Liz   It was me.

Jacqui *looks at her.*

Liz I think it was me.

Jacqui You?

Liz I forgot – I knocked them off the edge. And they broke, and I tried to pick them up . . .

Jacqui Liz . . .

Liz And I may have leaned on things . . .

Jacqui Just fill the kettle for us, will you?

Liz Oh . . .

She goes to the corridor door, then stops.

Only . . .

Jacqui *waits.*

Liz Yes . . .

She goes out.

Jacqui Dear Liz is in one of her flittering and squittering moods. What she means is that I'm being unkind to Kevin, but I *know* it was him, Shireen saw him, and you *have* to treat them just as you would anybody else, that's the absolutely basic principle.

She looks at the envelope, which she is still holding.

'Private and Confidential . . .'

Hilary Would you give it to me?

She stands up and puts out her hand for the envelope. **Jacqui** *goes on looking at it.*

Jacqui Have you shown this to Roy?

Hilary No.

Jacqui No, well, Roy's a wonderful man. I don't know about his private life, of course, that's nothing to do with me . . . But he *is* a lawyer, he *is* cautious – naturally, he has to be . . .

Hilary (*holding out her hand*)   Please.

Jacqui   And you're absolutely right to show it to Terry first. Sit down! I'll tell you something about Terry while we're waiting. Something you may not have realised. Sit down . . .

Hilary *reluctantly sits.* **Liz** *comes back in with the kettle, and plugs it in.*

Jacqui   He's a good man. (*To* **Liz**.) I'm telling her about Terry. (*To* **Hilary**.) I know, you see, because we've been in this together from the very beginning. We started the Campaign together! It was a kind of miracle. I was at rock bottom – we both were. Me in the middle of this truly ghastly divorce – Terry absolutely on his beam-ends.

Liz *watches them anxiously, uncertain whether to go or stay, whether to intervene or be silent.*

Jacqui   I'd just been at my solicitor's – I couldn't find a taxi – when suddenly the heavens opened. So there we were, sheltering in the doorway of this shop, both feeling sorry for ourselves – and we simply looked at each other – and that was it. We started to talk, and we went on talking for seven hours non-stop. My precious, it was the Sea of Galilee all over again. I said, 'You've just found your first disciple . . .' (*To* **Liz**.) You're like one of those maddening insects that can't make up their minds whether to come or go! (*To* **Hilary**.) Yes, and when we were starting the Campaign I wasn't only his disciple, I was all twelve apostles. One room, that's all we had then. Just the two of us, living on faith, waiting for it all to happen . . . (*To* **Liz**.) Liz, my sweetheart, you're scattering Nescafé over the floor! (*To* **Hilary**.) No, he's a good man. In fact I'll tell you something in confidence – he's a great man . . .

Liz *clashes the coffee-mugs together.*

Jacqui   Liz, sit down and let me do it! You're going to break something in a moment!

Enter **Terry** *through the main door with a bath-towel round his neck.*

Terry   Right, I've decided. Thought about it in the bath.

Shireen *slides her screen back.*

Shireen   Oh, Terry . . .

She gives him his letters. He crosses to his own office, looking at them.

Terry (*to* **Shireen**)   Call my old chum at Special Branch. (*To everyone.*) That leak – what does it tell us? Nothing. So, all right, we'll be good Scouts and give it back to them.

Shireen   And there's another one, a big one. Where is it?

Jacqui (*holds it up*)   I've got it.

Terry *goes into his office.*

Terry (*off, to everyone*)   Only we'll get some of our pals in the press round to watch us do it . . .

Shireen (*to* **Terry**)   And *she's* here!

Terry *emerges from his office without the towel, still looking at his letters.*

Terry (*to* **Shireen**)   Special Branch, number's on the pad. Inspector What's-his-name, prat with a moustache. *Who's* here?

Shireen   Her!

Terry *picks up the letter.*

Terry   And who screwed this up . . . ?

He looks up and sees **Hilary**. *A coffee-mug falls out of* **Liz**'s *hands and smashes.*

Liz   I'm sorry. I'm sorry.

She vanishes into the library.

Jacqui (*to* **Terry**)   Hilary. Roy's friend.

Terry   Right.

Jacqui   She came last night.

Terry (*cautiously*)   Hello, Hilary.

Hilary *smiles awkwardly.* **Jacqui** *is discreetly holding out the envelope to* **Terry**.

Jacqui   We've been having a little talk about things.

Terry   Oh, yes?

Jacqui   About the Campaign.

Terry   That's nice.

Jacqui   About you.

Terry   About me?

Hilary   I'm late for something . . .

She gets up. **Jacqui** *puts a restraining hand on her arm.*

Jacqui   But I've been persuading her to stay. Because I think you and she are going to want to have a little talk about things as well.

Terry (*takes in the envelope*)   What?

Jacqui *goes on holding it out, looking significantly at him.* **Liz** *appears in the doorway of the library.*

Terry   What's going on?

She continues to hold the package.

'Private and Confidential'? What's all this?

He looks from **Jacqui** *to the others.* **Hilary** *looks away.* **Liz** *vanishes. He opens the envelope and takes out a file. Inside the file is a stack of photocopied pages.*

Shireen (*to* **Hilary**) I told you!

Terry 'Home Office, secret. Mr K. Hassam . . .'

Shireen Oh – window shut!

Shireen *closes her screen.* **Terry** *looks at* **Jacqui** *again, then reads. Silence.* **Jacqui** *watches him significantly.* **Hilary** *gets to her feet again.* **Jacqui** *restrains her.* **Liz** *appears in the doorway of the library.*

Jacqui Aren't you? Going to want to have a little talk?

Silence. Then **Terry** *looks up.*

Terry Fellow I was in prison with won ten grand once at roulette. He said when they call the number, and you know it's yours, it's like as if time stops for a moment . . . You've died. You've gone to heaven . . . I think they just called my number.

He holds up the papers.

It's only the whole file! All the memos, all the briefings! Only the whole story, that's all, only the whole cover-up! Right, into battle! Shireen!

Shireen *opens her screen.*

Terry Get me Mike Edwards, BBC News! He's in a conference? – get him out of the conference! He's on a plane? – get him off the plane! No, hold on. Let's think this out . . . Get Roy first!

Shireen He'll be in court, Terry!

Terry Get him out of court!

Shireen *closes her screen.*

Terry Even Roy's going to say 'Let's go' on this one! We got you this time, Hilary! Got you good and nailed. Right, let's get it copied before anything happens to it . . . (*To* **Jacqui**.) I'll do it myself. Get the boys out of there.

Jacqui *goes out to the mailroom.*

Terry The fairies bring it – the fairies might take it away again . . .

Liz *(distressed)* Terry . . .

She makes anxious attempts to indicate **Hilary**.

Terry What – Hilary? I know.

He waves the file around in front of **Hilary**.

Terry *(to* **Hilary***)* I showed you the last one – I'm not showing you this one!

Liz No . . . no . . . !

Terry *(to* **Liz***)* No, nor you. All of us banged up we won't have no organization left. *(To* **Hilary***.)* Just go back and tell your chums in Whitehall – this time we're going to fry them!

Kevin *and* **Kent** *come in, propelled by* **Jacqui**.

Kevin What . . . ?

Terry *(to* **Kevin***)* Doughnuts!

Kevin Doughnuts?

Terry *gives* **Kevin** *money.*

Terry Six doughnuts.

He glances at **Hilary**.

Terry Seven doughnuts. Special treat. Help each other choose.

Kevin Why . . . ?

Terry Celebrating. Bit of luck. Few quid on a horse.

He bundles them out through the main door.

Kevin But . . .

Terry Only take your time. Look inside each

doughnut, make sure it's got a full load of jam.

He goes towards the mailroom with the file.

(*To* **Liz**.) You – back to work. Jacqui – likewise.

Liz *goes back into the library.*

Terry (*to* **Hilary**) You – sit there. Be with you in a moment.

He turns to go out, then stops.

Hold on . . . Shireen!

Shireen *opens her screen.*

Shireen They're just getting him, Terry!

Terry Who?

Shireen Roy!

Terry Right. Just tell me one thing, Shireen.

Shireen Yes?

Terry Where'd this come from? This didn't come in the post.

Shireen She *brought* it! She *brought* it!

Terry She *brought* it? *Who* brought it? (*To* **Hilary**.) *You* brought it? You're not . . . you're not in the Home Office?

Hilary No.

Terry No. Sorry. For one horrible moment . . .

Hilary But yes, I did.

Pause. **Liz** *emerges from the library.*

Hilary Bring it.

Pause.

Terry Where'd you get it, Hilary?

Hilary   I copied it. From the file.

Pause.

Terry   I thought you said...?

Hilary   I'm not. Now. I *was.*

Terry   In the Home Office?

Hilary   Yes.

Terry   Was in the Home Office till when, Hilary?

Hilary   Till this morning.

Terry   Till this morning?

Hilary   I've left. I've resigned.

Liz   Oh, no!

She claps her hand over her mouth.

Terry   You've resigned? This morning?

Hilary   About...

She looks at her watch.

... twenty-five minutes ago. I sent a note up to the head of my section. Then I came here.

Terry *gazes at her.*

Shireen   She comes in, she says, 'Where's Terry?' I say, 'He's out having his bath.'

Jacqui (*quietly*)   She was going to take it away again, my sweet.

Shireen   I go like, 'Sit down. Wait for him.'

Terry (*stunned*)   Oh, Hilary!

He sits down.

Jacqui   I *knew* what was inside as soon as I saw it.

Hilary   I was lying awake all night. I just started to

think about it. About what it must have been like when
he begged the police to help him, and they launched
into him as well, and he knew there was no one in the
world left to turn to . . . It just suddenly came into my
head, I don't know why. But then I don't know why I
hadn't thought about it before.

Terry   What are you doing to me?

Hilary   I got up and walked round the streets. I've
never done that before. I think it was about five o'clock.
Everything looked somehow very clear and sharp, and
completely . . . unreal. I felt slightly feverish. And terribly
excited.

*She picks up a piece of broken slimbread, and breaks it into
smaller pieces as she talks.*

I didn't know what I was going to do! I might have
been going to do *anything!* It was like being fifteen again
and feeling the summer on your skin and wanting to
take all your clothes off. Or all the words you mustn't
say. Did you ever have the feeling that there are all
these forbidden words inside your head, and they're red-
hot, and they're burning a hole through your skull?
They're shouting aloud inside you, and any moment
they're going to come bursting out. Suddenly, in the
middle of the maths lesson, or when you're having tea
with your family. You're just going to find yourself
saying them. Or you're standing on the platform in the
tube, and the train's coming, and you can feel the edge
of the platform kind of pulling you, and you think, 'The
one thing I mustn't do – the last thing on earth I *want*
to do . . . How do I know I'm not going to do it?'
There's you and there's all these things inside you that
may be going to do themselves . . . I walked all the way
into the office – I haven't had any breakfast! Then I
remembered we'd got the file you wanted. It just seemed
such a perfect fit. You wanted it, and we'd got it. So I
drew it out, and went to the copier on the floor below

. . . I thought about people opening the envelope. And
the pages sliding out. And the look on people's faces . . .

Terry   Two years, Hilary . . .

Hilary   I suppose it's a rather surprising thing to have
done, now I come to think about it. It's very surprising!
It's the most surprising thing I've ever done in my life!
The worst thing. The worst thing I could ever imagine
myself doing.

Jacqui   Oh, you poor love!

Hilary   No – it was so easy! I just put each page in
the copier, and closed the lid, and pressed the button.
And that's all there was to it!

Liz *laughs. She puts her hands over her face.*

Hilary   I suppose I'm making it all sound a bit mad,
but it wasn't mad in the slightest – it was perfectly
rational. I just suddenly felt I'd lived my entire life
keeping something shut away inside me. Shut away so
tight that I didn't even know quite what it was. It wasn't
me that was mad, it was the world – because a world
where half the things you know are things you mustn't
say is a mad world. And a world where no one remarks
on the fact is madder still . . .

Terry   Two years, though. Two years out of your life,
and no life to go back to afterwards.

Hilary   It's not because of anything *you* said. If that's
what's worrying you. I just . . . started to think about it.

Terry   OK, never mind two years. What about your
mum, though – what would your mum say if she knew
you was taking things from the people you work for?

Hilary   Yes . . .

She looks out of the window.

Terry   I know you haven't got a dad . . .

Hilary (*sharply*)   No, and I don't want one.

Terry   No, and I'm not dressing up as one.

Hilary   Anyway, they're not people I work for. Not now. That's all over. I went back to my desk and wrote a note to Mr Hollis. I just said I was sorry, but I couldn't do the job any more . . . He was a kind man, he liked me, he was bringing me on in the department . . . But it's very simple. We all know what happened. Why not say it?

Pause.

Terry   Right. So here's what you do, Hilary.

He puts the file back in its original envelope.

You put all this in one of them black plastic rubbish bags down the street. Not in our doorway, cause who knows? Someone else's. All right?

He pushes the envelope across the desk to her.

Then you go back to the office. You tell that nice boss of yours you been under a lot of strain, you need a break, would he please tear up the letter. Then you take a couple of weeks' holiday, you thank Christ there's still one or two complete fools around in this world, and you get on and work your way up to Permanent Under-Secretary. And if you ever get the feeling coming over you again, you just bung us a small contribution to the funds instead. Always much appreciated.

Hilary *looks at him, and smiles.*

Terry   Then when you *are* Permanent Under-Secretary, come back to us, and I won't give you no second chances.

Hilary *gets up.*

Hilary   Thank you. Jacqui's right. You're a good man.

Terry   Straight back, then, Hilary. No funny turns, no

am-I-aren't-I shall-I-shan't-I. So Shireen puts her headset
back, excitement's over. Liz goes back in the library and
finds us another good scandal instead out of the trade
papers and journals, like she done before.

Shireen *closes her screen.*

Liz   Lovely, though. While it lasted.

She goes back into the library.

Terry   So *what* you going to do, Hilary? Just tell me.
Just make sure we got it all straight in our minds.

She pushes the envelope back to him.

Hilary   I'm going to the Job Centre.

She goes out.

Terry   What have I done, Jacqui? What have I done?

Jacqui *jumps up, and picks up the envelope.*

Jacqui   I'll catch her on the stairs.

She goes to the main door.

Because she *could* be, couldn't she?

Terry   Could be what?

Jacqui   Ours. Our daughter. If things had been
different.

Terry   Wouldn't have been more than six, my love, if
so.

Jacqui   No, but sooner or later she might have met
some man. Thrown her life away. Because that's what
this is all about, you realise. She's besotted!

Terry   Is she?

Jacqui   Oh, one look at her! And Roy's such a rotten
devil!

Jacqui *goes out with the envelope.*

(*Calls.*) Hilary . . . !

Terry *turns to go into his office, then notices the slimbread that* **Hilary** *was breaking up. He starts to brush the pieces into the waste-paper basket, then realises that* **Liz** *has emerged from the library again. He indicates the desk.*

Terry Bit of clearing up. OK? Because I don't like to think what you been up to here, Liz.

Liz (*laughs*) No . . . I suppose that's why she came up and introduced herself to me.

Terry What?

Liz At that charity evening. I suppose that's why she made me introduce her to Roy.

Terry What are you talking about, Liz?

Liz Because we knew you.

Terry What do you mean?

Liz Nothing. Anyway, it doesn't matter, it's all over – you gave it all back to her . . .

Enter **Jacqui**, *holding the envelope. She throws it down on the desk.*

Terry What, didn't catch her?

Jacqui Caught her. She wouldn't take it.

Terry So now what?

Jacqui I told her we'd find a job for her.

She sits down at the desk and begins to work.

Terry A job for her?

Shireen *opens her screen.*

Shireen It's Roy! He's really cross! He was in the High Court! They've got him out!

Terry Yes, well, tell him . . . Tell him to go back in

again.

Shireen   Oh, no! He'll go mad!

She waits.

Terry (*to* **Jacqui**)   A job?

Liz   What – *here*?

Jacqui   Yes. Was that all right?

Terry   No, it wasn't.

Jacqui   Plenty of things she can do, my darling.

Liz   Oh, no! Oh, Jacqui!

Jacqui (*to* **Liz**)   For all of us . . .

Terry   Not all right at all.

Shireen (*into headset, apprehensively*)   Hello, Roy, listen . . .

She closes her screen.

Kent *comes in through the main door, laughing, holding a cardboard tray of doughnuts.*

Jacqui   What?

Kevin *follows him anxiously, mopping ineffectually at his face and clothes with the backs of his hands.*

Kevin   Jam . . .

Kent   Picks one up, looks inside, gives it a squeeze . . . out it comes, all over everything!

He demonstrates – and covers himself in jam.

Curtain.

Act Two

The same.

Scene One

Night. **Shireen** *is on the switch,* **Kevin** *and* **Kent** *are visible working in the mailroom.* **Jacqui** *is sitting at her VDU.* **Hilary** *is sitting on the other side of the same desk, trying to work. The door to the library is closed.*

Jacqui (*to* **Hilary**) Well, you know what Terry's like. He doesn't see what's in front of his eyes. And it's not just the cardboard boxes. It's those soggy paper plates with congealed food on them. And food isn't the only thing they leave on those plates. I realise they've probably no access to toilet facilities, but the plates they've been eating off – I mean, honestly! I'm not madly fussy or houseproud – we live in an absolute pigsty in Sunningdale – but the doorstep *is* how we present ourselves to the world.

Hilary I'll do it.

Jacqui Oh, my precious, certainly not. It's Shireen's job, but you know Shireen – all she ever does is smile. Terry simply doesn't back me up on this, it's hopeless. I try to keep the office running for him, but I can't do it if people know he's not behind me.

Terry *comes out of his inner office and stands looking at them.*

Jacqui Go away! We're talking about you!

Terry It's six o'clock. It's knocking-off time.

Jacqui It's quarter to six. You go if you want to. We're enjoying ourselves.

Terry I thought today was the newsletter?

Jacqui It is! I've done it!

Terry And the Hassam lobby? Definitely nothing we've forgotten?

Jacqui No! I told you!

Terry House of Commons? All our branches? All our tame MPs?

Jacqui Tell him, will you, Hilary? (*To* **Terry**.) I know you don't trust *me*.

Hilary (*to* **Terry**) I think it's all covered.

Jacqui We did it together! Don't fuss! Go back in there! Shut the door if you don't want to hear!

Terry Got to keep my ears open, my love. Check there aren't no plots or conspiracies hatching out here. Make sure we're still all one big happy family.

Terry *goes back into his office, but leaves the door open.*

Jacqui He should be in Special Branch.

Terry (*off*) I heard that.

Jacqui (*to* **Hilary**) Anyway, you're still working. This is your Hassam thing?

Hilary It's just the background. So Terry can make sense of that file.

Jacqui He's not going to do anything with that file, you know, my sweet.

Hilary He's thinking about it, isn't he?

Jacqui For three days? I've never known Terry think about a thing for three minutes.

They both look towards the door of **Terry**'s *office.*

Jacqui Silence.

Pause.

Hilary   Tina and Donna.

Jacqui   Sorry?

Hilary   Their names. The girls who sleep in the doorway.

Jacqui   Oh, you're so quick! Three days, and you know more about this place than I do!

Hilary   No – I just happened to run into them.

Pause. **Hilary** *works.* **Jacqui** *watches her.*

Jacqui   Actually we'd quite happily chuck up Sunningdale and find some little place in Chelsea or Kensington, but Poops has got to have somewhere to keep Pippy, and we can't stable a pony in the middle of Sloane Square . . . I feel bad enough about leaving the dogs all day, because I do think dogs have a right to a bit more out of life than two walks a day with a paid companion. Don't you?

Hilary *works.*

Jacqui   I'm talking too much. It's funny – I don't usually get on with brainy types . . . The house is far too big for us, though . . . Is Roy keen on pets?

Hilary   Roy? I've no idea.

Jacqui   It must be a tiny bit intimidating, having rows with a lawyer. Or don't you have rows?

Hilary   Not really.

Pause.

Jacqui   What does he think about your working here?

Hilary   I don't think he knows.

Jacqui   You haven't told him?

Hilary   Not yet.

Jacqui   You mean you haven't seen him?

Hilary *stops trying to work.*

Hilary Well, it's all quite complicated.

Jacqui Fenella?

Hilary Among other things.

Jacqui Oh, my sweet love! But he hasn't even phoned?

Hilary I've been out a lot.

Jacqui Honestly! Men!

Hilary Well ... and women.

Jacqui I mean, I know what it's like, believe me. When there's someone you love, and you can't live with them ...

Terry *comes out of his office.*

Jacqui I'll tell you when it's six o'clock!

Terry *hesitates, then goes back into his office. Pause.*

Hilary (*suddenly*) Yes, and you want to talk about them all the time, and say their name, and tell everyone ...

Jacqui And you have to keep biting it back ...

Hilary And you think you'll die if you don't say it just once ...

Jacqui Because you have to be terribly discreet and sensible.

Hilary And you can't believe it's not written all over you, and shining out of you.

Jacqui Oh, my poor precious!

Pause.

Hilary Perhaps we shouldn't be quite so discreet and sensible.

Jacqui   No, perhaps not.

Pause.

When did you meet those girls?

Hilary   Tina and Donna?

Jacqui   They're never around in the day.

Hilary   No. No ...

Terry *comes out of his office again.*

Terry   I don't care what time it is. It's Friday evening, and we're all going home. Come on, Shireen!

He bangs on the mailroom window and indicates his watch.
Shireen *slides her window back.*

Shireen   What?

Terry   It's the weekend!

Shireen   Oh, lovely!

Terry   So busy listening to these two rabbiting you never noticed.

Shireen *emerges from the switch.*

Shireen   I had my window shut! Honestly!

She goes out to the corridor.

Terry   What do you think, then, Hilary, end of your first working week?

Hilary   It's very nice. Everyone's very friendly. I've enjoyed it.

Jacqui   It's you, my sweet! You've transformed this office! Hasn't she, Terry?

Terry   Yes, when you think what it was like in here last week. Everyone shouting and screaming. Can't even remember now what it was all about ...

Kevin *comes in carrying his haversack, followed by* **Kent**.

Jacqui   *I* can.

Terry   Oh, yes.

Kevin *struggles to get something out of the haversack.*

Kevin   This is just something . . . Just something . . .

Kent   Come on, get it out.

Kevin   Just . . .

Jacqui   What – something for Hilary, is it, Kevin?

Hilary   For me?

Kevin   Just . . .

Jacqui   A bar of chocolate, yes, we can see.

Kevin   Just something . . .

Hilary   Oh, Kevin, you mustn't spend your money on me.

Kevin   Something . . .

Terry   So that's what he keeps in that bag of his. I've always wondered.

Kent *laughs.*

Terry   What?

Kent (*shrugs*)   Just laughing.

Terry   Anyway, that's a beautiful thought, Kevin.

Kevin   Something . . .

Hilary   Thank you, Kevin. It's really sweet of you.

Shireen *comes back from the corridor, putting her overcoat on.*

Jacqui (*to* **Shireen**)   Kevin's bought a bar of chocolate for Hilary!

Shireen   Ohhhh! Isn't that nice!

Kent *tries to pull* **Kevin** *away.*

Kevin Something...

Kent Come on, she don't want you hanging round all night.

Kevin Something...

Shireen Lovely weekend, everybody! Lovely weekend, Hilary!

Hilary Yes. And you.

Terry Night, Shireen.

Shireen *goes out.*

Kevin Something...

Kent Don't mess her about, Kevvy!

Terry So what are you up to this weekend, Kent?

Kent Me? Nothing.

Terry Oh, that'll make a change.

Kevin ... to mitigate the shortcomings of the office coffee.

Terry Oh, it's to mitigate the shortcomings. That's why he can't get the words out – they're all a yard long.

Hilary Anyway, I'm very touched.

Jacqui Now just leave her to eat it in peace.

Terry Night, then, Kev. Take care.

Kent *pushes* **Kevin** *out.*

Terry Don't wobble off the platform on the way.

Kent (*to* **Hilary**) See you Monday.

Hilary Me? Yes. Good night.

Kent *goes out.*

Jacqui   A bar of chocolate, though! I think you've made a tiny bit of a conquest there, my love.

Terry   What about old Kent? 'See you Monday, Hilary.' I've never heard him making fancy speeches before. Saucy bugger.

Hilary (*looks at her chocolate*)   It's books, usually.

Jacqui   What?

Hilary   In Kevin's bag. He goes out in the lunch-hour to buy them.

Jacqui   Oh, there's quite a little thing going on between you two, isn't there, my sweet!

Terry   Not careful we'll have Kevin and Kent murdering each other in there.

Terry *goes back into his office.*

Hilary   Well, if we really are all finishing . . .

She stands up and folds up her work.

Jacqui   I was just thinking . . .

Pause. **Hilary** *waits.*

Jacqui   What peculiar creatures men are . . .

Hilary   You mean . . . Kevin?

Jacqui   No . . .

Pause. The library door opens, and **Liz** *comes out. She sees* **Hilary***, and stops, all smiles.*

Liz   Oh, sorry.

Jacqui   What?

Liz   Nothing. I thought . . .

She goes back into the library.

Jacqui What *is* the matter, Liz, my sweetheart?

Liz Nothing . . . nothing . . .

Jacqui This is the umpteenth time you've done that today! You don't like the look of us?

Liz *smiles and closes the library door.*

Jacqui What with him popping out of there, and her popping out of here . . . It's like living in a shop full of cuckoo clocks . . . ! She always used to leave the door open – I don't know what's eating her . . . Of course she lives with some woman friend of hers. I can guess what *that's* all about, not that it's anything to do with me . . .

Pause.

Hilary Peculiar creatures. Men. You were just saying.

Jacqui Oh, yes. Don't you think?

Hilary What – Terry?

Jacqui Terry?

Hilary I thought you might be thinking of Terry.

Jacqui Yes. Or Pippy.

Hilary Pippy?

Jacqui Poops's pony. Although I'm not sure he counts as a man because he's been *done* . . .

Hilary *laughs.*

Jacqui What?

Hilary What people tell you and what they don't.

Jacqui How do you mean?

Hilary Well . . . No.

Jacqui What?

Hilary Nothing. Only you always say 'we'.

Jacqui   Do I?

Hilary   'We have this person who walks the dogs . . .
We're going to have the garden remade . . .'

Jacqui   Yes, well, Poops . . .

Hilary   Isn't she away at school?

Jacqui   Half-term – I told you.

Pause.

Hilary   Yes. I'm sorry. Forgive me.

Jacqui   Anyway, there's Pippy. And the dogs.

Hilary   And the cat.

Jacqui   Well, I *do* think of them all as 'us' . . .

Hilary   Of course. I'm sorry. Anyway . . .

She goes to the corridor door.

Jacqui   You mean I'm always asking about you and
Roy?

Hilary   Oh . . . No. Not at all.

Jacqui   You never say 'we'.

Hilary   Don't I? No . . . 'We . . . us . . .'

She laughs.

Jacqui   What?

Hilary   Strange words.

She goes out through the corridor door. **Jacqui** *stands up and
stretches, then opens the library door.*

Jacqui   Do *borrow* her!

She goes back to her desk and puts her things together to leave.
Liz *appears in the doorway.*

Jacqui   Well, you're being so funny about it! I don't

want to monopolise her. I told Terry she could work for both of us. He wouldn't have taken her on otherwise. It was hard enough persuading him as it was.

Liz   Jacqui . . .

Jacqui   Even though he *adores* her.

Liz   Jacqui, I can't bear this!

Jacqui   Why, what's the matter?

Liz   Nothing . . .

Jacqui   Can't bear what, though, my love?

Liz   Well . . . everything . . .

Jacqui   You look most peculiar.

Liz   No, it's just that . . .

Hilary *comes back from the corridor, putting on her overcoat.*

Jacqui   What?

Liz   Forget it, forget it.

Liz *goes back into the library.*

Jacqui (*to* **Hilary**)   Off, then, are you, my sweet?

Hilary   Unless there's anything else . . . ?

Jacqui   No, no. Off you go. It's been absolutely lovely having you here, my precious.

Hilary   Lovely being here. (*Calls.*) Good night, Terry! Good night, Liz!

Terry *appears from his office.*

Terry   Night night, then, Hil. Get your breath back. Big week coming up.

Liz *appears in the doorway of the library.*

Hilary   Yes. Good night, Jacqui.

Jacqui Have an absolutely super weekend.

Hilary I will.

Terry Don't do anything I wouldn't.

Hilary *goes out of the main door.* **Jacqui** *turns decisively to* **Terry**.

Jacqui Terry, listen . . .

Terry *looks at* **Liz**. **Jacqui** *looks as well.* **Liz** *disappears back into the library.* **Jacqui** *shuts the library door.*

Jacqui Hilary . . .

Terry What about her?

Jacqui You know what she's doing every time she gets half a chance?

Pause.

Terry No? What's she doing?

Jacqui She's writing some sort of report about the way the Home Office works. I had a look when she was out of the room today. Terry, my love, she's putting in everyone's names – all the people she used to work with. She's saying what part they all played in the Hassam thing. Did you know about this?

Terry No. No, I didn't.

Jacqui Well, you're going to have to be very firm with her, my darling. Because, Terry, if we did anything that got her into trouble . . .

Terry Listen, I feel just the same as you . . .

Jacqui The Home Office security people are going to interview her again tomorrow. They know something's up . . . You're *not* going to do anything silly with that file, are you?

Terry Aren't I?

Jacqui Terry, you *couldn't*! You *couldn't*! Not now we know her! Not now she's one of us!

Terry No . . .

Jacqui Terry!

Terry Yes, but she wants us to. She wants us to use it.

Jacqui But you know what'll happen! You said yourself!

Terry She don't care. She wants us to.

Jacqui You've talked to her about it?

Terry Long talk.

Jacqui When was this? I haven't seen you talking to her.

Terry Last night.

Jacqui I was here last night.

Terry After you'd gone. She come back to the office. Left her bag behind.

Pause.

What's that supposed to mean?

Jacqui What?

Terry That look?

Jacqui Terry . . . you have still got it?

Terry Got it? What, the file?

Jacqui Where is it?

Terry You don't trust me?

Jacqui I just want to see it.

He goes into his office.

(*Softly.*) I know you, my sweetheart.

He comes back holding up the file.

Terry   I gave it to her, my old love! You fetched it back!

Jacqui   Terry, she's in a very strange state!

Terry   Funny old state *you're* in, my love, never mind her.

Jacqui   Yes, but something's happened, I don't know what it is. I think she's probably had some truly ghastly bust-up with Roy. You know she hasn't even told him she was working here? You haven't said anything to her about . . . ?

Terry   What?

Jacqui   Us.

Terry   No? Why?

Jacqui   Something she said. I know it's silly, but I just feel we ought to be a bit . . . careful. Well, I remember the way Poops reacted when you first came out to Sunningdale. I don't think children want to know too much about what their parents get up to.

Terry   We're not her parents! Keep saying it to yourself! We're not her parents!

Jacqui   Yes, but I expect she's a bit soft on you herself, you see, my darling. She's terribly careful never to look at you. Haven't you noticed?

She goes out to the corridor.

(*Off.*) Well, even Poops has a funny thing about her father, I'm perfectly well aware of that, though she'd die rather than admit it to me.

She comes back with her overcoat, and moves towards the main door.

Anyway, all the girls still go a bit woozy when they see you, as you well know, and of course they do, because you're a very attractive man, and you're more than that, you're a great man, and I told her so, and don't you take advantage of it . . .

She looks at the file.

We shouldn't keep that in the office. What happens if we get Special Branch round with a search warrant again?

Terry   Still secret?

Jacqui   Well, it is.

Terry   Yes . . .

Jacqui   We're not leaving it here over the weekend?

Terry (*thinks*)   No . . .

He offers it to her.

Take it home with you.

Jacqui   Me?

Terry   Hide it away somewhere. Safe from them. Safe from me.

Jacqui   Aren't you coming?

Terry   Coming where?

Jacqui   Home!

Terry (*remembering*)   Oh, what, Poops – she's back for the hols?

Jacqui   You hadn't forgotten?

Terry   Course I hadn't forgotten.

He doesn't move.

Jacqui   What?

Terry   Nothing.

He pats his pocket.

Wallet. Go on down. I'll catch you up.

Jacqui She'd be so disappointed.

Terry I'm coming!

She goes out. He thinks, then pushes open the library door, still holding the file.

Liz . . .

Liz *comes anxiously out of the library.*

Terry You here for a bit?

Liz It's Friday.

Terry Tidying everything up for us?

Liz Just the usual.

Terry Right, so anyone wants to know where I am . . .

Liz You'll be away tonight.

Terry Old Poops. It's her half-term.

Liz I know.

Terry Can't be helped.

Liz No.

Terry (*thinks*) Just tell them . . . No, put it like this . . . No, say I'll phone them.

Liz Phone them, right.

Terry You'll lock up, then?

Liz Yes.

He opens the main door, and stands there for a moment, looking at the file he is holding.

Terry All getting a bit deep for me, this, Liz.

Liz (*laughs bleakly*)   All getting a bit deep for all of us.

Terry   Yes. Sorry about that.

She looks at the file.

Liz   It looks like a bomb, the way you're holding it.

Terry   What, this?

Liz   What are you going to do with it?

Terry   I don't know, Liz. I don't know.

Liz   Throw it.

Terry   Blow up a lot of things if I did.

Liz   Why not? Blow up everything.

Terry   People we know.

Liz   If we're serious about Mr Hassam.

Terry   Mr Hassam's dead. Other people aren't.

Liz   Also we didn't know him.

Terry   Makes a difference, Liz.

Liz   Does it?

Terry   Doesn't it?

Pause.

Liz   So you're taking it away?

Terry   Put it somewhere safe.

Liz   In Jacqui's house?

She laughs.

Terry (*ruefully*)   Right.

She holds out her hand for the file.

Give it to you?

Liz   Neutral territory.

Terry (*thinks*)   No, I'll put it back where it was.

Terry *takes the file back into his office.*

Dangerous things, bombs. Less they get moved around the better.

He closes his office door.

So you'll tell them, if they come?

Liz   Tell who?

Terry   Them.

Liz   Oh, them.

Terry   OK. You're a pal.

He goes to the main door.

Liz   And tomorrow night?

Terry   We'll see how it goes.

Liz   And Sunday night?

Terry   We'll see, tell them. We'll see.

Liz *sits down in* **Jacqui***'s chair, turns on the computer, and opens all the files that* **Jacqui** *has just closed. Then she goes back to the main door, opens it, and listens. The sound of the street door closing three flights below. She closes the door and goes into* **Terry***'s office. The main door opens, and* **Hilary** *looks in cautiously. She crosses to* **Terry***'s office and listens, then smiles to herself.*

Hilary   Wait! Don't come out till I tell you!

She turns away and quickly starts to undress, without taking off her overcoat. **Liz** *emerges from* **Terry***'s office, holding* **Hilary***'s file.*

Hilary   I said wait . . . !

She looks back and sees that it is **Liz***. She pulls the overcoat around herself. Pause.*

Liz   He's not here. He's had to go away for the night.

Hilary   No, I just came back to . . .

Pause.

Liz   Catch up on some work. Right.

Hilary   I'm sorry.

Liz   No, no.

Hilary *notices the file in* **Liz**'s *hands.*

Liz   I was fetching your file. Terry told me to look after it.

She goes to **Jacqui**'s *seat, and begins to work on* **Jacqui**'s *files.* **Hilary** *goes uncertainly to her own part of the desk.*

Hilary   And Terry's had to . . . ?

Liz   Go away somewhere. He said he'd phone. If anyone asked for him.

Pause.

Hilary   Thank you, anyway.

Pause.

It's very nice of you. I realise it's all rather . . . awkward.

Liz   Not at all.

Hilary   Well, it is.

Liz   Yes, but so's everything.

Hilary   Is it?

Liz   Don't you find?

Pause.

Hilary   Not always.

Liz   No?

Hilary   Not usually.

Liz   When you come back to catch up on your work?

Hilary   Yes.

Liz   Good. I'm glad.

She works.

Hilary   What are you doing?

Liz (*grins*)   Oh ... tidying up.

Hilary   But isn't that ... ?

Liz   What – Jacqui's? Yes!

Pause.

You mean, should we be messing around with Jacqui's things?

Hilary   No, I was simply wondering ...

Liz *works on, grinning.*

Liz   It's the newsletter. She won't use the spell-checker. I don't know why not. And she hates anyone else looking at what she's done – I always have to go through everything when she's not here. It's so silly – she knows perfectly well I do it. People are funny, aren't they. It can't go out like this, though. Do you want to see?

Hilary *shakes her head. Pause.*

Hilary   Just tonight?

Liz   He didn't know. He said he'd see how it went. (*Laughs.*) This is her appeal for funds. Listen: 'Come on all you affulent types ...'

Liz *laughs.* **Hilary** *does not.*

Liz   '*Affulent* ...' I can just see them, can't you? All our affulent supporters. At one of those lunch meetings that Terry has to go and talk to, probably. Somehow affable and flatulent at the same time, sort of burping benevolence.

Liz *laughs.* **Hilary** *does not.*

Liz Sorry. Sorry ... There are some things you can't tell people, though, aren't there. Some things you have to let them find out for themselves. Don't you think?

Pause.

Hilary Gone where?

Liz I don't know. Oh no, this is a classic! 'Let's make next month's appeal figures a real *banasa ...*'

Hilary Bonanza?

Liz I suppose. I had a wild picture of some sort of specially squashy banana.

Hilary You mean she's dyslexic?

Liz Or *disexic*. That's what she said in one of her editorials. 'Hold on to your seats chaps the poor old Ed's a raging disexic.' Sorry! I keep all these things to myself usually.

Hilary Disexic ...

She smiles slightly, and relaxes enough to button up her shirt.

Liz Quite funny, though, having someone who's disexic to edit the newsletter. Don't you think? It's the same with the accounts. She won't use the spreadsheet, I don't know why not. It makes Terry so cross! She does them all by hand, on odd bits of paper. Then she takes them off to a *little man* down in Sunningdale. She's got all kinds of *little men* working away for her down there. It's like Snow White and the Seven Dwarfs. Anyway, her little man lays them out and makes them look all right – I don't know how – she never lets anyone else see them – certainly not me – I don't think even Terry – she keeps them under lock and key ...

She pulls at the drawer in the desk in front of her to demonstrate.

You see? Quite funny, having someone who can't do accounts to do the accounts. Don't you think?

Hilary   I get the impression she lives with someone.

Liz *laughs.*

Hilary   Or perhaps not all the time. She's very mysterious about it. She never refers to him directly. I thought possibly he was . . .

Pause. **Liz** *waits.*

Hilary   I don't know. Someone else's husband. Or the gardener, or something.

Liz *resumes work.*

Hilary   No?

Liz *gets up. She fetches the wire coat-hanger that* **Terry**'s *shirt was on. She holds it up for* **Hilary** *to see, smiling.*

Hilary (*puzzled*)   Coat-hanger?

Liz   Haven't you ever picked a lock?

Liz *laughs, and picks the lock of* **Jacqui**'s *drawer.*

Hilary   Listen, I don't think we should . . .

Liz   Yes, we should, if she keeps it locked. Don't you want to find out about all our little mysteries?

Hilary   Liz, don't . . . don't . . .

Liz   I've done it!

She takes the drawer out and puts it on the desk.

Aren't we awful?

Hilary (*seriously*)   Yes, we are.

But she watches, fascinated, as **Liz** *goes through the contents.*

Liz   I hate looking in someone else's things! Don't you? I just want to run out of the room . . .

She searches avidly among the contents, and pulls out a small child's painting.

'My Mummy'! Aren't we horrible?

She takes out some picture postcards.

More Poops. 'I'm having a brill time. The food is yucky. Inez was sick in Fiona's ski boot. We all hate the French.'

Hilary *puts her envelope down, and looks in the drawer. She takes out an exercise book.*

Liz   Two odd gloves ... Four old pennies ... Receipts ... VAT invoices ...

Hilary   These are the accounts ...

Liz *takes out a spiral-bound shorthand book and looks inside it.*

Liz   I think this is the payroll ...

Hilary   Subscriptions ... covenants ... There doesn't seem to be very much money coming in ...

Liz   Do you want to know what we all earn?

Hilary   No, thank you.

Liz   It's funny what people don't want to know about.

Hilary   I don't see how we keep going on this income ... I suppose she was ... having some kind of affair with him. Was she? Is that how it all started ...

Liz *(laughs)*   I'll make us some coffee.

She goes to the kettle and switches it on.

Hilary   And now he feels he can't just push her out ...

Liz   Anyway, never mind.

Hilary   Nothing to do with me.

Liz   Listen, why don't we leave all this nonsense?

She turns off the kettle.

You look a bit tired. We'll go out and see a film.

She quickly puts everything back in the drawer.

Hilary   Why never mind?

Liz   Nothing. You could come back to my place afterwards – we could have something to eat.

Hilary   Well, that's very kind, only I've got to do various things . . .

Liz   Come on! Jacqui told me to borrow you!

She fits the drawer back into the desk.

It's funny, really. She keeps all this mess inside her desk . . .

Liz *slams the drawer home.*

. . . but you should have seen her when she found those broken biscuits!

Hilary *looks away.*

Liz   Sorry!

She clamps her hand over her mouth.

Lock it up again.

Hilary *watches her sombrely as she tries to relock the drawer with the coat-hanger.*

Liz   It opened like a dream – I don't know why it won't . . . Doesn't matter – she'll think she left it like this herself . . .

She hides the remains of the coathanger in the waste-paper basket under some newspapers.

On second thoughts . . .

She takes it out again, and goes out with it into the corridor. She reappears inside the mailroom, holds up a waste-paper basket, grinning, and puts the coat-hanger into it. She returns putting on her overcoat.

Kevin's! She won't look there . . . Terrible pair we are!

She switches off the computer, and puts **Hilary**'s *coat around her shoulders for her.*

Liz You went such a lovely red, though! When Shireen said.

Hilary Said what?

Liz About the biscuits.

She propels **Hilary** *towards the main door.*

Liz Anyway, never mind. Don't worry about it! But I think you'll find he's usually got things to do at the weekend.

Hilary You mean . . . ?

Liz Anyway, there's always Chrissie's room. The girl I share with. She's away a lot at the weekend . . . Oh, the file!

She runs back and fetches it.

We'll take it with us. We can look after it together.

They go out.

Curtain.

Scene Two

Day. **Shireen** *is on the switch.* **Kent** *and* **Kevin** *are in the mailroom.* **Hilary** *is working at her desk. The door to the library is open.*

Jacqui *enters through the main door.*

Jacqui That doorway . . . ! (*To* **Hilary**.) Hello, my precious.

Hilary (*coolly*) Hello.

Jacqui Lovely weekend?

Hilary Thank you. And you?

Jacqui Funny smell in here ... Oh, you know, family life ... What *is* that smell ... ? No, we all had a lovely time.

Shireen *slides back her screen.*

Shireen Oh, Jacqui, that Steve person rang for Terry again ...

Jacqui Yes, yes – only don't go away, Shireen. Something I want to say to you.

Liz *appears in the doorway of the library.* **Jacqui** *puts her handbag down on her desk.*

Jacqui (*to* **Hilary**) Are you all right, my love?

Hilary Fine.

Jacqui Only you look a bit funny somehow. Doesn't she, Liz?

Liz *laughs.*

Jacqui A little *beaky*. Nothing's happened?

Hilary No.

Jacqui Not something over the weekend ... ?

Hilary No.

Jacqui No, well, it's probably just the weather. Or the smell ...

Liz What smell?

Jacqui Can't you smell it?

Shireen What's it like, Jacqui?

Jacqui Different. Now, Shireen!

She takes off her overcoat.

I come in on a freezing Monday morning to start what's obviously going to be a horrendous week, what with the Hassam thing, and our great lobby coming up tomorrow, and what do I find?

She takes her overcoat out through the corridor door.

Shireen (*to* **Liz** *and* **Hilary**)   Oh, no! I forgot the doorway again!

Liz (*to* **Shireen**)   I'll do it!

She goes to the main door. **Jacqui** *comes back without the overcoat.*

Jacqui   I find that doorway downstairs in the most incredible state.

Liz   I'm going, I'm going!

Jacqui   I mean *clean.*

Liz (*stops*)   Clean?

Jacqui   No cardboard, no cans, no congealed food on paper plates – nothing. So thank you, Shireen!

Shireen   Oh, well . . . I do *try* to remember, Jacqui.

Jacqui   Good. Well done! We've got the week off to a lovely start for once. And Kent's not picking his nose. Kevin's not scratching himself . . .

She stops, looking at something under her desk.

Shireen   What – the smell?

Liz   What sort of smell is it?

Shireen   Nice? Nasty?

Jacqui *bends down and picks up two used cardboard plates under her desk.*

Liz   What?

Shireen   What is it, Jacqui?

Jacqui   Spaghetti. Apparently. In tomato sauce.

Liz   Oh, no.

Shireen   Oh, Jacqui, how awful!

Jacqui   Shireen, my love, I didn't mean take the rubbish out of the doorway and put it under my desk!

Shireen   I didn't!

Jacqui   That's an absolutely cretinous thing to do!

Shireen   It wasn't me, Jacqui, honestly!

Jacqui   I've got this muck all over my hands now!

She drops the plates in the waste-paper basket and rushes out of the door to the corridor.

Shireen   I didn't put anything under her desk!

Liz   Don't worry.

Shireen   But whatever I do it's wrong! I say I didn't do the doorway – she goes mad! I say I did do it – she goes madder still!

Liz   What does it matter?

Shireen   It's so unfair!

The phone buzzes.

'Thank you, Shireen' – then two minutes later it's as bad as last week . . . (*Into headset.*) Hello, OPEN . . .

Liz (*to* **Hilary**)   *You* did it?

Hilary   Me? The doorway? No.

Liz   Another mystery.

She looks in **Jacqui**'s *handbag.*

Hilary   What – her keys?

Liz   Get the drawer locked up! That'll be the next thing!

Jacqui *comes back in, even angrier than when she went out.*

Jacqui   Where is it?

Liz *moves away from the handbag.*

Liz   What?

But **Jacqui** *is looking at the door, not the handbag.*

Jacqui   The coat-hanger!

Liz   The coat-hanger?

Liz *and* **Hilary** *look at each other.* **Jacqui** *bangs on* **Shireen**'s *screen.* **Shireen** *opens it.*

Jacqui   Shireen, my sweet . . .

Shireen *(into headset)*   Hold on . . .

Jacqui   There was a wire coat-hanger hanging here on Friday. Where is it?

Shireen   Oh, Jacqui, I don't know, I haven't seen it . . . A wire coat-hanger?

Jacqui   Yes! I need it, you see.

Shireen   You need a coat-hanger?

Jacqui   To unblock the lavatory.

Shireen   Oh, no!

Jacqui   I won't describe the state the room's in.

Shireen   Oh, poor Jacqui, what a morning! Have you asked the boys?

Jacqui *turns to look at the mailroom.* **Kent** *and* **Kevin**, *who have stopped to watch events in the main office, quickly resume whatever they were doing.*

Jacqui   Only of course it won't be them. It's never

them. It's never anyone.

Hilary (*to* **Jacqui**)   I don't think it's Kevin or Kent . . .

Jacqui (*to* **Hilary**)   Don't worry, my precious – I'm not going to eat them! But *no one* in this office will ever admit *responsibility* for anything. It absolutely *enrages* me.

She goes out of the corridor door again, and appears in the mailroom.

Shireen   It's Kevin, isn't it . . .

She emerges from the switch to watch.

He's always doing funny things with things. Oh, she's really, really going for him! You can't watch, can you, only you kind of can't stop . . .

Hilary (*to* **Liz**)   We'll have to tell her.

Liz   Wait! Wait!

She searches through **Jacqui**'s *bag.* **Shireen** *gazes at the mailroom.*

Shireen   It's in his bag, it's in his bag . . . He won't show her! He's hanging on for dear life . . . !

She sees what **Liz** *is doing.*

Shireen   What?

Liz (*laughs*)   Nothing.

Shireen   That's Jacqui's.

Liz   I was just looking for something.

Shireen   What's going on? I don't know what's going on here this morning!

Liz *takes her hands away from* **Jacqui**'s *bag, shamed by* **Shireen**'s *scrutiny.*

Shireen   I don't know what Hilary's going to think.

Hilary (*looking at the mailroom*)   She's found it.

Shireen   Oh, no!

Jacqui *is gesturing with the remains of the wire coat-hanger that she has extracted from* **Kevin***'s waste-paper basket.*

Shireen   In his bag?

Hilary   In his waste-paper basket.

Jacqui *disappears from the mailroom.*

Hilary   Liz, we'll have to say . . .

Shireen (*to* **Hilary**)   Yes, because you've never seen Jacqui like this before, have you. Oh, poor Hilary! (*To* **Liz**.) She thinks we're all mad! (*To* **Hilary**.) She'll have a go at you next! Won't she, Liz?

Liz   Probably. If we don't get everything else right . . .

She puts her hand into **Jacqui***'s handbag again while* **Shireen** *is talking to* **Hilary***.*

Shireen   You were so thick together last week, but that won't stop her! So were Jacqui and Liz once! Weren't you, Liz? She falls out with everyone, that woman, it's a shame, because if it's not like friendly here, I mean, what's the point? You'd rather leave, wouldn't you, you'd rather do audio . . .

Enter **Jacqui** *from the corridor.*

Jacqui   Shireen . . .

Liz *moves away from the handbag.*

Hilary (*to* **Jacqui**)   That coat-hanger . . .

Jacqui (*to* **Hilary**)   One moment, my love . . . Shireen, is it you who blocked the lavatory?

Shireen   Blocked the lavatory? Not me, Jacqui, I haven't been in there.

Jacqui (*to* **Liz**)   There's no need to go snittering and jittering! I don't want to hold a court of inquiry, I don't want to blame anyone. I simply want to find out what happened so we can stop it happening again.

Shireen   It was probably just Kevin, you know what he's like.

Jacqui   Yes, but whatever Kevin gets up to in there, I don't think he'd put a sanitary towel down the loo. Let alone two sanitary towels together.

Shireen   Oh, Jacqui, no!

She puts her hands over her face, embarrassed.

Jacqui   Oh, Jacqui, *yes*! Now, Shireen . . .

Hilary   I think this is probably my fault.

Jacqui (*to* **Hilary**, *irritated*)   Oh, don't *you* start, my darling! It's maddening enough when Liz does it! I'm not going to be angry with her. I just want to *know*. (*To* **Shireen**.) Now listen, my precious . . .

Hilary   Tina and Donna.

Jacqui   What?

Hilary   The two in the doorway. I said they could sleep in here last night.

Shireen   Oh, no!

Liz (*laughs in surprise*)   Sorry . . . The smell . . . Sorry . . .

She hides her face in her hands.

Shireen   And the plates . . .

Hilary   I should have mentioned it before . . .

Jacqui   I don't understand.

Hilary   Those two girls.

Shireen   They slept in here!

Liz   On the floor?

Hilary   There was a frost last night.

Jacqui (*to* **Hilary**)   What are you saying, my love?
You're not saying that you ... *invited* them in?

Liz (*laughs*)   Sorry ...

Jacqui (*to* **Liz**)   You knew about this, did you?

Liz (*laughs*)   No!

Jacqui (*to* **Hilary**)   So you took it upon yourself ...?

Hilary   I told them to be out this morning before
anyone arrived.

Jacqui (*smiling with anger*)   My honey ... My dear sweet
girl ...

Hilary   I'm sorry. I should have made sure they'd left
the place tidy.

Jacqui   I know you've been working in this office for
all of a *week*, my darling ...

Hilary   There was no one here to consult, so I had to
make a decision ...

Jacqui   Yes, but I don't imagine you'd have invited
people in off the street in your *last* place of employment!

Hilary   But if you've got an organisation that believes
in openness ...

Terry *comes in through the main door, holding a number of
clean shirts on hangers.*

Jacqui (*to* **Hilary**)   No, my darling! No! No! No!

Hilary   ... we can't really keep our doors locked ...

Jacqui   No! Listen to what I'm telling you! *No!*

Hilary   ... when there are people outside who may
die ...

Jacqui   *No!* Quite simply – *no!*

Shireen (*to* **Terry**)   Those girls! They spent the night in here!

The phone begins to buzz.

Hilary (*to* **Jacqui**)   Listen . . .

Jacqui (*eyes closed*)   No! I'm sorry! No! No! No!

Terry (*calmly*)   OK, end of argument . . .

Jacqui (*to* **Hilary**)   No! You see? No! No!

Terry   I said end of argument. Shireen, you get back on the switch, the phone's going. Liz, this don't concern you.

Shireen *returns to the switch.*

Shireen (*into headset*)   Hello, OPEN . . .

She closes the window. **Liz** *goes back into the library.*

Terry   Right, back to work. All over and done with. No need to go on about it because it's not going to happen again.

Terry *unhurriedly hangs up his shirts.*

Jacqui (*to* **Hilary**)   Last night? What do you mean, you let them in *last night*? Last night was Sunday!

Terry   Never mind about that . . .

Jacqui   No, but what was she doing here?

Hilary   I came in. I had some work to do.

Jacqui   Work? What work?

She turns over the papers on **Hilary**'s *desk.*

Hilary (*closes the file*)   Just some work of my own.

Jacqui (*opens it*)   This is your file. These are the things you sent to Terry.

Hilary   I'm annotating it. I thought we could hand out

copies at our lobby tomorrow.

Jacqui   But Terry said he left it in his office.

Shireen *slides back her window.*

Shireen   Terry . . .

Jacqui (*to* **Terry**)   You said you put this back in your office.

Terry (*to* **Jacqui**)   Hold on, hold on . . .

Shireen (*to* **Terry**)   It's Peter someone.

Terry (*to* **Shireen**)   Not now, love.

Shireen *waits, interested.*

Terry (*to* **Jacqui**)   Let's take this nice and gentle.

Hilary   Liz gave it to me.

Jacqui   Liz gave it to you? But this is ridiculous! (*Calls.*) Liz! (*To* **Hilary**.) When did she give this to you?

Liz *emerges from the library.*

Hilary   Over the weekend.

Jacqui   Over the weekend? Last night? You were both here?

Hilary   On Friday night.

Jacqui *looks from one to the other.*

Jacqui   I don't understand. What's going on?

Hilary   I think we ought to publish this material.

Jacqui   And you were going to do it behind all our backs?

Hilary   No, I thought we should all talk about it and decide together.

Jacqui   Oh, *did* you, my darling?

Terry   Fair enough. We got to get it thrashed out sooner or later. Why not now? It's going to take all morning, though, so let's get ourselves sat down before we start.

Hilary *sits down at her desk.*

Terry   Liz . . .

Liz *sits.*

Terry (*to* **Jacqui**)   And you, my love.

Jacqui *reluctantly sits.*

Shireen   Terry . . .

Terry (*to* **Shireen**)   I said, not now. Tell him.

Shireen *reluctantly closes her window.*

Terry   Right.

He sits down himself.

Let's have a proper debate. Are we going to publish Hilary's file or aren't we? I call on Hilary to speak first, tell us what *she* thinks. Go on, then, Hilary.

Jacqui (*to* **Hilary**)   Who gave you the keys?

Hilary   The keys?

Jacqui   To this office.

Hilary   No one.

Jacqui   No one? What do you mean, 'no one'?

Hilary   I had a set.

Terry   *I* gave them to her. Last week. Right – Hilary.

Hilary (*to* **Jacqui**)   I don't know what you're worrying about. I wasn't here with *him*.

Jacqui   With Terry?

Hilary   You know I wasn't. At least, I *assume* you know

I wasn't. Since he was with you. Wasn't he?

Jacqui   What do you mean? Why should he be here?

Hilary   Why should he be here? Because this is where he usually is at night.

Jacqui (*puzzled*)   Yes . . . ?

Terry   Never mind all that. Just tell us about this file of yours, Hilary. How can we publish it without dropping you in it . . . ?

Hilary (*to* **Jacqui**)   I'm just saying – Friday night, Saturday night, last night – he *wasn't*.

Pause.

Jacqui (*quietly*)   I'm going out for a walk. I don't feel very well.

She goes out through the main door.

Hilary (*to* **Terry**)   I'm sorry. But you *weren't*!

Terry (*quietly, not looking at* **Hilary**)   I'd better take her her coat. She'll catch her death out there this morning.

He goes out to the corridor.

Liz (*to* **Hilary**)   Well done!

Hilary   I didn't mean it like that!

Liz   Are you all right?

Terry *reappears from the corridor, carrying* **Jacqui***'s coat.* **Liz** *melts back into the library.*

Hilary (*to* **Terry**)   Anyway, she'd have had to face up to it sooner or later.

Terry   Right . . . Though I don't know why sooner or later always has to mean sooner.

Terry *goes out of the main door.*

Hilary   Wait . . .

Hilary *runs out after him.* **Liz** *comes out of the library.*
Shireen *opens her screen.*

Shireen (*to* **Liz**)   My know-all sister! 'But Shireen,' she goes, 'nothing ever happens in that office!'

The phone buzzes.

(*Into headset.*) Hello, OPEN ...

Liz *opens the main door, then stops.*

Terry (*off*)   ... Hil, I been ringing your number all weekend! I rang you seven times ... !

Liz *shuts the door again.*

Shireen (*into headset*)   No, he's out ...

Liz *discreetly returns to her search of* **Jacqui**'s *handbag.*

Shireen   No, she's out – they're all out – there's only Liz ...

She turns to **Liz**, *and calls.*

Shireen   Liz!

Liz *quickly takes her hands out of* **Jacqui**'s *bag.*

Shireen (*to* **Liz**)   Oh, sorry ...

She goes back to the main door, and looks cautiously out.

(*To* **Liz**.) Only it's that man in television about the lobby tomorrow ...

Liz *grins and shakes her head, and goes out.*

Shireen (*into headset*)   No, sorry – *she's* going out as well – they've all gone mad this morning ... !

Kent *runs in from the corridor door towards the switch, holding* **Kevin**'s *haversack.*

Kent   Hey, Shireen! Kevin's got this picture of you in his bag with no clothes on!

Kevin *comes in from the corridor door.*

Kevin   No! No!

He chases **Kent** *ineffectually around the desks.*

Kent   What? That one where they're doing it on the motor-bike! You said it looked like Shireen!

Kevin (*desperately*)   I didn't . . . !

Shireen *emerges from the switch.*

Shireen   Now don't you two start!

Kent   It's Kev! He's got all these wicked books!

He pulls magazines out of the haversack to show **Shireen**.
Kevin *struggles to stop him.*

Kevin   Give me . . . Give me . . .

Kent   Look at him! He's a crazy man!

Shireen   Yes, well, don't tease him.

Kent   I'm not, I'm cheering him up! Well pissed off, he was!

Kevin   Give me that . . .

Kent   Did something weird with her coat-hanger, didn't you, Kev? Old Jacqui was giving him all kinds of grief.

Shireen   Look, will you two stop messing around!

Kent   Hey, look at this one, Shireen . . .

Kevin   Give me that . . . Give me that . . .

He lunges at **Kent**, *who jumps on to the desk to keep the magazines out of* **Kevin**'s *reach. He tramples back and forth over the files and papers, while* **Kevin** *flaps ineffectually around his knees.*

Kent   No, she'll love it, Kev! She'll know you fancy her!

Kevin   I don't . . . I don't . . .

Kent   You *don't* fancy her? Shireen, Kev don't fancy you no more! What, it's Hilary now, is it, you wicked man?

Shireen   Get out of here, the pair of you! I've had nothing but messing around ever since I came in this morning!

The phone buzzes.

I'm sick of it! Now my phone's going . . .

She starts back to the switch, but is distracted by **Kevin***'s dislodging* **Jacqui***'s handbag.*

And that's her bag!

Kevin *grabs at the bag to save it, and the contents empty over the edge of the desk on to the floor.*

Kent   Oh, now you done it, Kevvy!

Kevin *and* **Shireen** *try to recover the contents of the handbag.* **Kent** *tips the contents of the haversack over their heads. The phone goes on buzzing.*

Kent   Here you are, you bad boy! Bums and bazoombas everywhere! Hey, no, get this one!

He throws the haversack away and recovers one of the magazines from the desk. **Liz** *and* **Hilary** *enter through the main door and stop short at the sight.*

Kent   I think this one's Hilary! Look! Look! Down over the desk, darling . . . !

He becomes aware of **Liz** *and* **Hilary***, and becomes instantly inert.* **Kevin** *and* **Shireen** *straighten up as well. The phone stops buzzing. Silence.*

Hilary *(quietly)*   Get off there, will you please, Kent. That's my desk. Those are my papers.

Kent *gets down.*

Shireen   Just half a chance, that's all they need, these two!

Liz *picks up some of things that* **Shireen** *and* **Kent** *have recovered.*

Liz   Is this all out of Jacqui's bag?

Shireen   They're always coming in here making trouble!

Liz *gets down on the floor, pushing the magazines aside. She hands* **Hilary** *some papers.*

Liz   This is out of your file . . . But where are her keys? There should be some keys.

Shireen   I told them! I begged them!

Kevin, *still kneeling, is holding the magazines he has recovered. He looks round for the haversack.* **Hilary** *takes the magazines out of his hands.*

Hilary   Thank you, Kevin.

Kevin   Oh . . . Oh . . .

Hilary (*to* **Kent**)   These are yours, are they?

Kent *shrugs.* **Kevin** *looks at* **Hilary**'s *feet.*

Kevin   I won't . . . I don't . . . I won't . . . I don't . . .

Hilary   Just a moment, Kevin. I'm talking to Kent.

Kevin *looks up, mouth open.*

Hilary (*to* **Kent**)   I said, these are your magazines, are they, Kent?

Kent (*blankly*)   No.

Hilary   So what are you doing with them?

Kent   Found them.

Hilary   You found them. Oh. Found them where?

Kent   Lying around.

Hilary   Where – in the office?

Kent   Don't know.

Shireen   He goes, 'Look at these, Shireen!'

Hilary   So whose are they, Kent? Not Shireen's?

Kent *shrugs.*

Hilary   Mine? Liz's? Kevin's?

Kent *shrugs.*

Kevin   I think . . .

Hilary   Now, Kent, I know Terry's out. I know I've only been working here for a week. But there are some strange things going on in this office, and I've a pretty shrewd idea what's happening in that mailroom for a start. So let's all agree – no more harassment and no more bullying. Yes? Take this stuff away, then, Kent, and look at it in private, if that's the best you can manage, but don't ever bring anything like it into the office again.

She throws the magazines down on the desk in front of **Kent**, *and wipes her hands with a tissue.*

Hilary   Now we've all got a lot of work to do . . .

Kevin   In all fairness . . .

Hilary *(slightly impatiently)*   What is it, Kevin?

Kevin   In all fairness . . .

The main door begins to open.

Jacqui *(off)*   I don't want to know! All right? I simply *don't want to know*! I don't want to think about it . . . !

Jacqui *comes in, followed by* **Terry**. *She goes straight out to the corridor to hang up her coat without looking at the others.*

Terry   *Now* what's happening? The Christmas party?

Kevin   No . . .

Terry No. Right. So let's get some work done this morning.

Kevin I was just . . .

Terry Back in the mailroom, Kevin.

Kevin *obeys.*

Terry And you, Kent.

Kent *turns to go.*

Hilary (*to* **Kent**) Yes, and take these with you.

She picks up the magazines and gives them to him.

Terry Hold on. What's all this?

Liz Nothing.

Hilary It's all over.

Terry What are them mags?

Hilary Nothing!

Jacqui *comes back in from the corridor.*

Terry (*to* **Jacqui**) Nothing. That's what they're all doing.

Jacqui *shrugs, turns on the kettle, and fills a mug of hot water to wrap her hands around.* **Kent** *moves towards the corridor door with the magazines.*

Terry Nothing. Well, that sounds all right.

Shireen *sobs.*

Terry Hold on a moment, though, Kent.

Kent *stops.*

Terry Shireen don't look too happy about it all.

Shireen I don't want to work here any more.

Terry You what?

Shireen   I don't want to work in this kind of office! I
don't want to get all upset! I just want to know what
I'm supposed to do, and get on and do it. You say like,
'We're talking about secret things, you mustn't listen.' So
all right – I don't listen. You say like, 'We're all going
to be in trouble.' All right – so we're all going to be in
trouble! I don't mind! You tell me – I'll do it! I just
don't want people like being horrible all the time!

She goes out to the corridor.

Terry   Now, listen, Shireen, my darling. I don't know
what's been going on in here . . .

She comes back holding her overcoat.

Shireen   I know people don't always agree. I know
they've got sad things in their life. *I* don't always agree.
I've got sad things in *my* life. But I don't go round like
telling everyone and spoiling things for them.

Terry *puts his arm round her.*

Terry   Come on, Shireen . . .

*She pushes **Terry** away.*

Shireen   If people can't get on I don't think they
ought to like argue and make trouble for everyone. I
think they just ought to like put on their coat and go.

She puts her coat on. **Terry** *sits down in **Jacqui**'s chair and
calmly raises his hand.*

Terry   Not so fast, Shireen. I want to get to the
bottom of this. Let's hear from Kent. He's the expert on
nothing. What sort of nothing's been going on here,
Kent?

Kent *shrugs.*

Kent   Don't want to work in that room no more.

Terry   Oh. You don't want to work in that room no
more. So why's that, then, Kent?

Kent Don't want to work with *him* no more.

Terry You don't want work with Kevin? Why don't you want to work with Kevin?

Kent Just don't.

Terry Just don't. All right, Kent. So what you want me to say? Can't take Kevin out of there, can I, because what else can he do? Can't take *you* out, because what else can you do?

Kent *shrugs. The phone begins to buzz.*

Kent Go on the switch.

Terry Go on the switch? You want to go on the switch?

Kent *shrugs.*

Terry Funny, isn't it. First time I ever asked you something and you knew the answer. Well, that's a crying shame, my friend, cause the answer's wrong. No, you can't go on the switch. OK?

Kent Buzzing.

Terry Yes, and it's going to go on buzzing, I'm afraid, Kent.

Jacqui (*sharply*) Where's my bag?

Kent So why can't I go on it?

Terry Hold on, Kent. Jacqui's bag . . .

He picks it up from the floor where **Kevin** *and* **Shireen** *left it, and hands it to* **Jacqui***.*

Terry Right, that's one problem solved. (*To* **Kent***.*) Now, why can't you go on the switch . . . ?

He bends down again automatically to pick up something else he has noticed on the floor. It's one of **Kevin**'s *magazines. He looks at it. The phone stops buzzing.*

Terry   Oh. I see. That's what it's all about.

He throws the magazine down on the desk.

Now, listen, Kent. I don't like this kind of muck. If I was in the Home Office I'd have it all seized and burnt. Funny, coming from me? OK, laugh away, but there's a limit to everything. Everything? Everything. So, Kent, old son, drop all that garbage in the bin.

He waits while **Kent** *puts the magazines he is holding into the black plastic bag lining the waste-paper bin.*

Terry   Right. Now. Listen, Kent . . .

Jacqui   Someone's been going through my bag! All the things are mixed up and broken!

Hilary   Your bag got knocked off the table. We had to put everything back as best we could.

Jacqui   I can't bear people touching my things! (*To* **Terry**.) Get away from my desk! Get away! Go on! Out!

Terry *gets up.*

Jacqui   They haven't been into my drawer . . . ?

She shoves **Terry** *aside, and yanks at her drawer. It opens without resistance – comes right out in her hand and scatters the contents everywhere.*

Jacqui   Oh *no*! It was *locked*! I left it *locked*! I keep it *locked*! Which of you did this? Which of you broke into my drawer? (*To* **Kent**.) This was you, was it? Or was it Kevin? Was this with the coat-hanger? It was both of you!

Hilary   It was me. I did it on Friday evening. I wanted to see what you'd got in there. It was very stupid and very wrong of me. I shouldn't have done it. I'm sorry.

Jacqui   You?

Liz   Well, me, actually.

She laughs.

And I put the coat-hanger in Kevin's waste-paper basket afterwards.

Hilary   We did it together.

Jacqui   Together? Together? What have I ever done to you? What have I ever done to either of you?

Terry (*calmly*)   Now, let's take this very slow and very calm. Let's all see if we can somehow get this rusty old aeroplane back on the ground again . . .

The main door opens, and **Roy** *enters. They all turn to look at him. He stops short at the sight of them all assembled.*

Roy   Oh . . . More participatory democracy?

Terry   Right.

Roy   Admirable.

He advances into the room and places a typescript on the desk.

Secrecy in the legal profession. My report. I promised I'd bring it in.

Terry (*preoccupied*)   OK, Roy. Thanks.

Roy   So . . . everyone except Kevin. And me.

Terry   Sit down. Join in the fun.

Roy (*declines*)   I'll leave you with a written contribution instead.

He takes an envelope out of his pocket, and places it on top of the report.

Terry (*picks it up*)   What's this, Roy?

Roy   A personal note.

Terry *opens it and reads it.*

Roy   Well, I imagine you can dispense with *my* services now, can't you?

Terry   Oh, I see . . . No, we'd be very sorry to lose you, Roy, you know that.

Roy   But since you've appointed a full-time professional consultant of your own . . . (*Formally.*) Hello, Hilary.

Hilary (*formally*)   Hello.

Roy   And since you even did *that* without needing any advice from me . . . Without even asking me for a reference, which is a little curious, since I knew the applicant personally. Without so much as telling me you'd done it. I only found out over the weekend. (*To* **Hilary**.) From one of your former colleagues. Ironically enough.

Terry   Roy, can we talk about this some other time?

Roy   Of course.

He picks up the file from **Hilary**'s *desk and begins to look through it. The phone begins to buzz. No one moves.* **Roy** *looks up, first at the switch, then at* **Shireen**, *who has not moved.*

Roy   Oh, I see. Things are obviously changing around here. Your new consultant is plainly taking the organisation in hand.

Terry   We're busy, Roy.

Roy   Internal matters?

Terry   Off you go, then, old lad.

Roy (*looks through the file*)   This is what you're all talking about, is it?

Terry *closes the file up and takes it out of* **Roy**'s *hands.*

Roy   Oh – secret?

Terry   I'll be in touch.

Roy *laughs, and goes to the door.*

Roy   She's certainly making her mark. I could have told you. If you'd asked me.

Terry   Right. Cheers.

The phone stops buzzing.

Roy   Perhaps OPEN's not quite the right name any more. How about SHUT?

Roy *goes out.* **Terry** *keeps the file in his hands.*

Shireen   You see? It used to be nice here, it used to be friendly. They said at the agency, 'You'll like it, it's a very friendly office. It's not like advertising or anything, it's only like politics, but it's very friendly.'

She moves to go.

Terry   Wait a moment, Shireen. Where were we?

Kent   Why not?

Terry   Why not what?

Kent   Why can't I go on the switch?

Terry *(calmly)*   Hold on, Kent. Let's just get this other business sorted out first. Now, Jacqui . . .

Jacqui *is studying the magazine that* **Terry** *looked at earlier.*

Jacqui *(to* **Terry**, *holding the magazine)*   Rather appropriate, my sweet. He's having her across the desk.

Terry   Now come on, love . . .

Jacqui   I wonder why you did it on *my* desk instead of yours. I wonder if you know yourself. There's something very twisted hidden away there.

Terry   I don't think I know what you're talking about.

Hilary *(quietly)*   Well, we *do* know what she's talking about. And it's true.

Terry   Hilary . . .

Hilary   No, but if we believe in openness . . .

Jacqui (*to* **Terry**)   I think you've found a real disciple here.

Jacqui *puts all the bits and pieces out of her drawer into her handbag.*

Hilary (*to* **Terry**)   You and Jacqui, for instance. I think we should be told clearly what the arrangement is between you two, so we all know where we stand.

Jacqui   Oh, don't worry about *me*, my precious.

Hilary (*to* **Jacqui**)   No, we *all* need to know. All of us. (*To* **Terry**.) And about the arrangement between you and me.

Terry   Right. OK. Now . . .

Hilary   It's a difficult situation for me to accept. It's probably an even more difficult one for her. But if we know what it is then we can at least try.

She looks at the floor. **Jacqui** *goes out of the corridor door.*

Hilary   I know it's not easy to talk about this. It's not easy for any of us. But it's what you said, that first evening. You said we were making a city where all the houses had walls of golden glass. Transparent gold.

Jacqui *comes back with her overcoat.*

Hilary   Inside the houses people were living all kinds of different lives, with all kinds of different arrangements amongst themselves. Some very *comic* arrangements – that's what you said. But nothing hidden. Everything visible.

Jacqui   This is the Book of Revelation? Yes, I've heard all the Revelation bit, all the heaven bit. So why don't you do it in front of us all? On the desk. Now. Why not? It's not quite high enough for comfort, I know that from my own experience. Though I have to admit that was some years ago. You could perch yourself up on the files again, the way you did before. Or how about using the accounts? They're all yours now.

Jacqui *throws all the paperwork that she had in her drawer down in front of* **Hilary**.

Terry (*to* **Jacqui**) Let's talk about this, shall we, before we do anything too hasty . . .

Jacqui (*to* **Hilary**) You want to know why I gave you a job here? Because I thought you were a kind of daughter. You want to know what he's going to be thinking when he's got you sitting up on the accounts? The same.

Pause. **Hilary** *glances at* **Terry**, *then she looks back at the floor.*

Terry Jacqui, my love . . .

Jacqui What do you feel about all this, Liz? Shireen, how about you? Let's *all* talk about it. Or Kent. Yes, what are *your* feelings about all this, Kent, my sweet?

Kent (*shrugs*) Go on the switch.

Pause. **Terry**'s *temper suddenly goes. He slams the file down on the desk.*

Terry No! I told you! No! Got that? No!

Pause.

Hilary Anyway . . .

Terry (*to* **Kent**) You want to know why not? All right, Kent, I'll tell you why not. Because you haven't got the brains. See? Because you haven't got the style. Right? So you'll just have to go back in the mailroom with Kevin. And don't tell me you don't want to work with Kevin. Tell *him* – tell Kevin what's wrong with him. Kevin . . . !

Terry *jumps up and runs out to the mailroom.*

Liz   Oh no! Not Kevin!

Jacqui   Why not? Bring everyone down.

Shireen   It was so nice in here! It was so friendly!

Terry *comes back, dragging* **Kevin**, *knocking envelopes out of his hands, banging him into doors and tables.*

Terry   In here, Kevin! Nothing hidden? Right! Nothing hidden, then! So. Kent don't want to work with you no more, Kevin. Go on, Kent – why don't you want to work with him no more? Tell him!

Terry *shakes* **Kevin** *about in front of* **Kent**, *who shrugs and shuffles.*

Hilary   I don't see how this is going to help.

Terry (*to* **Hilary**)   Oh, don't you? So that's *your* nerve gone! (*To* **Kent**.) Tell him!

Jacqui   No, but it's pathetic, taking it out on Kevin!

Terry (*to* **Jacqui**)   And there goes yours! (*To* **Kent**.) Tell him! (*To* **Jacqui**.) And I'm not taking it out on Kevin, I'm taking it out on Kent, I'm taking it out on all of you, cause you got to listen to it. (*To* **Kent**.) Tell him!

Kent *shrugs.*

Terry   OK, Kevin, I'll tell you why Kent don't want to work with you. He don't want to work with you because he don't like you. He don't like you because you can't talk properly and you can't walk properly and you can't do your proper share of the work. And he don't like being lumped together with you cause that means we think he's just as useless as what you are. And he's right – that *is* what we think. OK, Kevin? OK, Kent?

Terry *lets go of* **Kevin**. *He begins to simmer down.*

Terry OK, Jacqui? OK, Hilary?

Hilary *sits down in her chair, silenced.* **Jacqui** *buttons her coat.*

Jacqui (*to* **Hilary**) At least you'll get the newsletter properly spelled. You have to keep writing to all the branch secretaries. They'll never send you anything otherwise.

Terry Right, that's it, folks – the show's over. Anyone who's going – go. Anyone who's staying – back to work. (*To* **Kent**.) You're going, are you? Coat? I'll get it for you. What about you, Kevin? Staying? Going?

Kevin Staying, staying.

Terry Back in there, then.

He bundles **Kevin** *out into the corridor.*

Terry (*to* **Liz**) And you. You got work to do.

Liz *retreats into the library.* **Terry** *returns from the corridor with* **Kent**'s *coat.*

Terry Right. Out. P45? In the post.

He bundles **Kent** *unceremoniously out of the main door.*

Shireen Terry, can I just say like, well . . .

Terry No. Out.

He holds the door open for her. **Shireen** *goes.* **Jacqui** *collects up her things.*

Terry People take what you say, they twist it round, and then they throw it in your face. Six years it took to put all this little lot together. One morning to blow it all apart again.

Jacqui (*throws down the key*) The key to the drawer. I expect someone's going to need it. (*To* **Terry**.) I couldn't spell. But I did manage to make the books balance. Six years, and never a moment's trouble with the books.

Terry   *You* don't have to go . . .

Jacqui *goes out.*

Terry   Hang on, love, hang on . . .

Terry *follows her out. Pause. Then* **Hilary** *collects up all the papers that* **Jacqui** *threw down in front of her.* **Liz** *emerges cautiously from the library.*

Liz   Suddenly – crack! Like a thunderstorm. I just wanted to put my head under the covers.

Hilary   As soon as we've got the lobby out of the way I'm going get started on these accounts . . .

She turns over the pages of **Jacqui**'s *exercise books.* **Liz** *sits down in* **Jacqui**'s *place, and tries to fit the drawer back into its slot.*

Liz (*laughs*)   And you! You were so angry! You went a lovely deep red again, like the wallpaper in that Indian restaurant we went to!

The expression on **Hilary**'s *face makes her stop laughing. She puts the drawer down.*

Liz   Look, don't start feeling guilty! You were right to say all that! And it's a good thing she's gone – you know it is! She was useless. She just put everyone's back up . . . Shireen and Kent would have gone anyway, sooner or later . . . Listen, I expect now you'll have things to do next weekend . . .

Hilary (*bleakly*)   Will I?

Liz   I mean, I assume . . . well . . . you know . . .

Hilary   I assume that this time he'll at any rate tell me.

Liz   But if you *do* ever want someone to talk to . . . Or somewhere to stay . . .

Hilary Yes. Thank you . . . These accounts. I suppose she was balancing them with her own money, was she? I suppose that was the great secret.

Liz (*shrugs*) I don't know. I've never thought about it.

Hilary *looks at her in amazement.*

Liz What?

Hilary You never wondered where the money came from?

Liz *laughs.*

Hilary All the things in life we never wonder about!

Liz It'll be all right. Don't worry. I'll help with the books. We'll do them together! We'll manage somehow!

Hilary I don't think we will, actually. Not without Jacqui's money. I think we're finished.

Liz We've still got us. We've still got you and me!

Hilary And Kevin.

They turn to look. Beyond the glass **Kevin** *is standing wobblingly on a chair, struggling with something on a high shelf. A mass of papers slips out of his hands and scatters.*

Liz And this!

She holds up the file.

Hilary Yes . . .

She takes it and looks at it thoughtfully.

Liz What's he going to do with it?

Hilary You mean what are *we* going to do with it?

Liz Oh, I see. But if Terry won't . . . ?

Hilary We'll do it ourselves.

Terry *comes slowly in and stands saying nothing. The collar of* *his jacket is turned up against the cold, and he is slowly rubbing his hands together, not looking at them.*

Terry   Sorry about all that. Either I should have been better than I was, or else I should have been worse. Excess of moderation, that's where I went wrong.

Hilary   It was Jacqui's money, was it?

Terry   I don't know.

Hilary   You never asked?

Terry   Who looks in the back of the clock, if the clock's going?

Hilary   Yes, well, I think our Hassam lobby tomorrow may be the last thing we do.

Terry   Bad as that?

Hilary   So . . .

She holds up the file.

Terry   What?

Hilary   Get it copied. Hand it out. At the lobby.

Pause. **Terry** *sits down in* **Jacqui***'s old place.*

Terry (*seriously*)   Look, Hil . . .

Hilary (*to* **Terry**)   How many copies shall we do?

Terry   OK, Hil, cut your own throat – I can't stop you. Put the knife in my hands – I won't do it, and that's that. The old fellow with his son in the Bible – yes. Me – no.

Hilary   I know what she said. But you're *not* my father, and it's not your decision.

Terry   Now come on, Hil. We got to be sensible about this.

Hilary (*holding the file*)   Terry, they kicked him to death.

Terry   They'll knock the life out of you, too, Hil.

Hilary   Why does it matter about me, if it doesn't matter about him?

Terry   Why? Same reason as it always is when something matters more than something else. Cause you're here and he's not. Cause you're close and he's distant.

He picks up the drawer, and knocks the dust out of it.

Right. Back to work.

He puts the drawer back into the desk.

Hilary   I don't accept that argument.

Terry   You don't have to accept it.

Hilary   But we do have to make a decision.

Terry   I've made it.

He takes the file out of her hands, tosses it into the drawer, and slams the drawer shut. The phone begins to buzz.

Moderation, Hil. Moderation. All right? (*Into phone.*) Hello, OPEN . . . She's not here. She's gone home. You want the number . . . ?

He goes into the switch.

Liz (*to* **Hilary**)   So?

Hilary   So – ourselves.

Liz   How?

Hilary *glances at* **Terry**, *then takes the file out of the drawer.*

Hilary   Same way as I did before.

She takes the file into the mailroom. **Terry** *emerges from the switch.*

Terry   What's worse, Liz – when people won't do what you tell them, or when they do?

Liz *glances towards the mailroom, where* **Hilary** *is setting to work at the copier.*

Liz   I suppose we'll find out.

Terry   We're not going to let her do it, are we, Liz? Don't want to put her away, do you?

Liz   She's helping Kevin with the copier.

Terry (*abstracted*)   Or maybe you wouldn't mind. Half of you would. But then there's another half of you underneath. Top half tidying the desk. Bottom half kicking the legs away. Bit of that in everyone, though.

Liz   Even in her?

Terry *follows her gaze towards the mailroom. They watch* **Hilary** *as she copies the file.*

Terry   I don't know, Liz. You look in through the window. You think you know what's going on . . .

Liz   Transparent gold . . .

Terry   I told *you* about it once.

Liz   Yes.

Terry   No secret.

Liz   Or do you wish you'd pulled down a few blinds?

Terry (*thinks*)   I don't want to pull down the blinds, Liz . . . No, maybe one. We all need to pull down one blind. One window covered over somewhere . . . Anyway, something'll turn up, don't you worry.

Liz   Will it?

Terry   Always has, Liz, always has. I walk into this café. There's this nice lady. Just got her divorce, and half the shares in the family investment trust . . . And off we go again.

Hilary *comes out of the mailroom, carrying the copy she has* *made, and the file concealed beneath it.*

Terry   So let's get this place cleaned up. Kevin!

*He fetches **Kevin***'s coat, and takes it to the mailroom.*

Terry   Here, put your coat on. Little job for you.

Hilary *quietly shows **Liz** the copy she has made.*

Liz   What are you going to do with it?

Hilary *puts the file back into the drawer.*

Hilary   Have we got an address for Terry's friend on BBC News?

Liz   Mike Edwards?

Hilary *takes the address book back to her place.* **Terry** *emerges from the mailroom, followed by **Kevin**.*

Terry   Sorry about the aggro I was giving you earlier. Won't happen again.

Kevin   No, I'm somewhat gratified that other people ... occasionally have to say difficult things.

Terry   OK. Now I want you to get this bag of filth out of here.

*He pulls out the rubbish-bag in which **Kent** dumped **Kevin***'s magazines.*

Terry   So ...

*He looks at **Hilary**. She is busy addressing an envelope. He glances at **Liz**, puts a finger to his lips, then quietly opens the drawer, takes the file out, shows it to **Liz**, and puts it into the rubbish-bag.*

Terry   Off you go, then, Kev. Drop it all on someone else's doorstep. And don't remember which doorstep it was.

Kevin *goes towards the main door.*

Hilary   Wait a moment, Kevin.

Kevin *stops. She puts the copy she made into the envelope she has addressed.*

Terry   No, something'll pop up from somewhere. Bound to. Feel it in my bones.

Hilary (*gives the envelope to* **Kevin**)   Put this in the post, will you?

Kevin *goes out of the main door with the envelope and the sack of rubbish.* **Liz** *gives a little laugh.* **Terry** *looks at her, and smiles, and puts a finger to his lips to warn her. She puts a hand over her mouth, to stop herself laughing, and glances at* **Hilary**, *who smiles.*

Terry   Right, start all over again. Only this time . . .

He locks the drawer.

I'll keep the key.

Curtain.

La Belle Vivette

A Note on the Adaptation

Zola, looking back on what he regarded as the moral swamp of the Second Empire in France from the healthier highlands of the Third Republic that succeeded it at the end of the 1860s, traces the history of the decade with magisterial dismissiveness through the career of a prostitute. Nana, in the magnificent novel which bears her name, rises from call-girl to actress to serious *cocotte*, sinks to common streetwalker, rises again to the ranks of the grandest *grandes cocottes* of all, then declines once more to salutary disfigurement and early death. She symbolises the corruption that runs through the society of the Second Empire, as Zola sees it, from the depths of the gutter to the supposed heights of the old Catholic aristocracy. She both satisfies and embodies its taste for pleasure and ostentation. Her profligate indolence is sustained by the huge new vulgar entrepreneurial energies of the age, by the surges of money pumped into its bloodstream like adrenalin from its reckless speculation and gambling. This tale of galloping depravity Zola places against a musical background, which provides the novel with a kind of theme-song. And the music he chooses is Offenbach's *La Belle Hélène*.

He doesn't mention the composer by name, and the opera itself is fictionalised, but the circumstances identify it clearly enough. The story begins on the first night of *La Blonde Vénus*, at the Théâtre des Variétés, where *La Belle Hélène* opened in 1864. Like both *Hélène* and Offenbach's first big success six years earlier, *Orphée aux enfers*, it is a flippant joke at the expense of classical mythology. Zola gives a characteristically vivid and thoroughly-researched account of a working theatre of the time, with its elaborate stage machinery and its all-pervading smell of coal-gas from the complex gasoliers that lit the stage with newfound brilliance. This is one of the great pleasures of the book – and he got a lot of his information direct from Ludovic Halévy, the co-author of *Hélène*.

The theatre makes the perfect starting-point for the story because of its traditional connections with prostitution; the fictitious proprietor of the Variétés insists on referring to it as his brothel. Nana is launched upon society by her appearance in the title role of the new show; out in front, watching the new star, are assembled all the characters who will become her victims. The audience represents a wide social spectrum:

> Paris was there – literary Paris, financial Paris, pleasure-loving Paris – a lot of journalists, a few writers, men from the stock market, more whores than respectable women; a strikingly mixed crowd drawn from all walks of life, spoiled by the same vices, with the same fatigue and the same fever written in their faces.

The music, to Zola's ears, sounds entirely suitable for Nana's 'working-class voice' – it was 'kazoo music, an echo of the fairground'. And at the dénouement of the novel, the grand ball after the cynical wedding that represents the culmination of Nana's career of corruption, the band plays the 'gutter waltz' from the show that launched her. It goes through the tottering great house like 'a dirty laugh ... some breath of carnality off the street ...'

Zola was not alone in his contempt. A subsequent success of Offenbach's, *La Grande-duchesse de Gerolstein*, was actually banned by the Republican government. Whether you share this moral horror or not, Offenbach's music does seem to reflect many of the aspects of the world that had come into being in the eighteen years after 1852, when Louis-Napoléon got himself proclaimed emperor (and then, remarkably, secured democratic ratification of his appointment by a landslide plebiscite).

It was a period of huge, if uneven and unsustained, economic expansion in France, when the new men with

the new money set the pace. Cock of the walk now,
lamented the Goncourt brothers in their journal, are
'boors and bounders, Lyons silk-weavers turned
millionaires, stagedoor stockbrokers'. Haussmann,
identified like Offenbach with everything that was later
deplored about the age, was tearing down the old Paris
and driving the great boulevards through it. He built the
sewers and gave the city its first clean water supply,
which ended the scourge of cholera. He created a world
of luxurious new streets, properly paved and lit by gas.
But the cost was terrible. Tenants had no protection,
and rents soared from month to month. People displaced
by the colossal programme of demolition were forced
out, like refugees from a war-zone, to the edges of the
city, where they lived, according to the Minister of the
Interior's own report, 'deprived of all resource, with
neither clothes nor bread . . . in such a state of
destitution that they would die of hunger if private
charity or public benevolence did not come to their
assistance.' Does some faint familiar echo of this stir in
our own recent past?

Haussmann, incidentally, had a very direct influence
upon the theatre. In 1862 he made way for the gigantic
new Place du Château-d'Eau (now de la République) by
pulling down the 'Boulevard du Crime' – the Boulevard
du Temple, the traditional street of theatres. (It had
earned its sobriquet because many of them specialised in
bloodthirsty melodramas – one actor reckoned that he
had been murdered in various ways during the course of
his career some 27,000 times.) Two of the big theatres
migrated to the Place du Châtelet, where they face each
other still like a pair of great beasts – the Châtelet and
the Théâtre de la Ville. But the smaller theatres joined a
migration westwards. The exquisite little jewel-boxes, the
bonbonnières bourgeoises, which remain the home of the
boulevard theatre in Paris today, are scattered along the
same street, the westward extension of the old
'Boulevard du Crime', though it changes its name as it

goes, from the Boulevard St Denis to the Boulevard Montmartre, and on beyond to the Boulevard des Italiens. This boulevard system was the line of the old city fortifications. A boulevard originally meant a street established on a demolished *Bollwerk* or bulwark, and the three great rings of theatres in Paris are all built on the line of successive defence systems. For once swords actually have been beaten into ploughshares. And perhaps there was something symbolic about this in the 1860s, because the French army turned out to be something of a ploughshare itself when it was put to the test at the end of the epoch.

Offenbach himself was a real man of the Second Empire. He was of German-Jewish descent, like many of the new men – born in 1819 in Cologne, where his father was cantor at the synagogue. (He took his name from his father's birthplace, Offenbach-am-Main, just outside Frankfurt.) His father moved the family to Paris, in the hope of finding a more liberal attitude to Jews, and the son studied the cello at the Conservatoire. He converted to Catholicism as a young man, but retained his Rhineland accent, and used to sign himself 'O. de Cologne'. He was dandified, witty, and obsessively hard-working. He was not only the composer of his shows – he was the entrepreneur who produced them. His life is a story of money as much as of music. He raised it, lost it, made it, lost it again on cards and women. His first backer was Henri de Villemessant, the newspaper proprietor who founded *Le Figaro*, and who had also bankrolled the city's first department store. The boom economics of the period are reflected in the sheer scale of Offenbach's commercial success – particularly of the two Greek pieces. *Orphée* set a new standard of financial achievement in the theatre. 'The great success of a piece these days,' said the Goncourts, 'is to create the customer who comes back, ie the man who sees *Orphée aux enfers* twenty times.' And with the production of *La Belle Hélène* in 1864, said Saint-Saëns, 'opera-madness

and the collapse of good taste began . . . Paris took leave
of its senses; everyone's head was turned. The most
respectable women tried to outdo each other in singing
Amour divin, ardente flamme.'

Since the original formula was such a success, it may
seem presumptuous to look askance at it now, and
wilfully wrong-headed to modify it for the present
production. The librettists, Meilhac and Halévy, plainly
knew their business; they wrote the book for several
more of Offenbach's pieces, including two more big
successes – and went on to provide Bizet with the text
of *Carmen*. The old *Hélène* has been frequently revived,
and become a great favourite in many parts of the
world; a Russian friend of mine told me that it was the
show she remembered being performed most regularly of
all in the Soviet Union.

But, while the music sounds (to my ears, if not to
Zola's) as fresh and delightful as ever, the book seems to
me to have mouldered over the years. The lyrics are
witty, and use French with a delicious untranslateable
crispness that I can only envy. Between the numbers,
though, come long dialogue scenes. This combination is
the traditional form of the *opéra comique*, which is an
early version of musical comedy rather than of opera
proper. Spoken dialogue in operas and musicals always
seems to me a painful letdown at the end of a musical
number – a sudden descent into the grey and now
strangely artificial everyday world, as when the television
lights are turned off at the end of some public occasion.
The dialogue scenes in *Hélène* are particularly leaden,
and are heavily cut in most modern productions. They
cannot be excised completely, though, because the plot,
such as it is, depends upon them. Their inanition comes
in part from a lack of dramatic movement in the overall
story: Paris and Helen are destined for each other by
the gods – they duly fulfil their destiny. It's true that
fate needs a little human assistance, and is also an
amusing excuse for human inclination. But there is little

room left for struggle, conflict, uncertainty – all the elements that are normally required to bring even the least serious story to life.

One of the things that gave the writing colour at the time was the familiarity of its reference. The intolerable riddles competition in Act One, for example, and the game of goose in Act Two, would perhaps have been more amusing to an audience who knew that they were a respectfully irreverent reference to the taste of the Emperor and Empress for party games. Some texture must also have derived from the audience's familiarity with the detail of the original myths. Presumably everyone still knows the outlines of the story of Helen and her abduction by Paris. But how many people in an average audience these days would understand Helen's line, which became a catchphrase at the time, 'Oh, Father, look on your child with a favourable beak'? It must by now have slipped many people's recollection that she was the offspring of the union between Leda and the Swan. Or that the Leucadia to which Orestes urges despatching spoilsport husbands was the island where disappointed lovers traditionally threw themselves into the sea? More damaging even than our fading knowledge of the classical world is our fading respect for it. In the middle of the nineteenth century Offenbach's flippancy had a certain piquancy, even the power to shock. One of the leading critics of the day attacked *Hélène* as a 'sacrilege, a desecration of antiquity'. Zola describes *La Blonde Vénus* as 'Olympus dragged into the mud, a whole religion, a whole poetry jeered at . . . A fever of irreverence seized the literate audience of the first performances; legend was trampled underfoot, the ancient images broken.'

It's difficult now to feel much trace of this excitement; irreverence, particularly towards the classics, has become routine. Alexander Faris, Offenbach's biographer, identifies the tone of the two operettas as what in England is called high camp, and places it in the same

tradition as Restoration comedy. I take his point, but
can't help feeling that at times the height of the camp
wilts discouragingly low. You wouldn't be particularly
surprised if Agamemnon turned to the audience and
said, 'Titter ye not.' Once again, though, it seems to me
that there is a divergence between the words and the
music, which is highly theatrical and frequently parodic,
but not really camp in any sense. It is vigorous, often
erotic, and always melodically downright.

The question of reference is fundamental not only to
the texture of the piece, but to its whole structure. The
original audience must have seen their own world as a
kind of foreground to the action. The very facetiousness
of the piece was a reference in itself, to the cocky
cynicism of the times. Now this foreground has vanished
into the scene-dock of history, and all *we* see is the
thinly painted backcloth.

So I've shifted the setting from classical Sparta to
Second Empire Paris, which is what (it seems to me) the
music itself cries out for in every bar. My story runs
parallel to the original one, but I've tried to tell it so far
as possible through the music itself, with the minimum
of dialogue. To this end I have reprised various
numbers, sometimes directly, sometimes with variations
in the lyric, and I have imported the Bellini parody
from an earlier work, *Ba-ta-clan*. I have also exchanged
the power of the gods and destiny for the efforts of the
human will and the laws of the market. With
nineteenth-century Paris instead of ancient Greece
painted on the backcloth, however sketchily, perhaps we
can supply a foreground from our own experience.

I also had another objective in mind. Even if this is
not the music of the fairground, as Zola suggested,
neither is it the music of La Scala or the Palais Garnier.
Hélène was not presented at the state-subsidised Opéra-
Comique, the official home of the genre. It was done
commercially, with private venture capital, in a small
commercial house. It is boulevard theatre in the most

literal sense – done on the boulevard and for the 'boulevard' – the disparate but homogeneous world that took its pleasures there. Siegfried Kracauer, in his book *Offenbach and the Paris of His Time*, says that at the Variétés everyone knew each other, and that 'there existed between the men about town and the actresses such an intimacy that the stage and the auditorium formed a single whole. As a result of this intimacy the audience had no hesitation in speaking out or freely exchanging witticims; an actress catching a remark on the wing that reached her from the front row of the pit would break off in the middle of a speech and burst into peals of laughter. In fact the only point of playing the part as she saw it was as a way of achieving ends completely alien to her profession. The entire audience was magnetised by the flux emanating from this perpetual interaction . . .' The whole atmosphere was remote from the respectful rituals of the modern opera-house, and I have tried to find a way of suggesting this intimacy between audience and performers.

The enterprise in which my characters are engaged is not party games, but the creation of an operetta – and one not entirely unlike *Hélène* itself. It is of course an entirely fictitious version of the event – but there are good precedents for this, and not only in Zola. Meilhac and Halévy's original was a fictitious account of the classical stories, and is particularly unfair to Menelaus, who in the *Iliad* emerges not as the traditionally feeble cuckold that they have made him into, but as one of the Greeks' most ferocious and feared warriors. (It's sometimes forgotten, too, that as a result of the ten-year-long war with Troy he succeeded in regaining Helen; in the *Odyssey* Telemachus finds them both back in Sparta some nine years after the war has ended, living together in apparent contentment.) But then the classical stories themselves were fictionalisations of the oral myths, which were themselves – well – fictions. Whether, in the green depths of this infinity of mirrors, some real prince ever did abduct some real queen, no one knows.

My version does have at least some distant affinities with verifiable history. Offenbach did not, like M. Berger, appear in his own work, but the original Helen, Hortense Schneider, bore some slight resemblance to Vivette. Zola's version of her, the Nana who couldn't sing audibly, and who simply swayed back and forth in time to the music in a revealing dress, is a gross libel. Schneider was a trained and experienced singer, who had a long and successful career in comic opera. But, like many actresses at the time, she did lead a colourful private life; she was the intermittently faithful mistress of one of the most famous of the *viveurs*, the duc de Gramont-Caderousse, who was working hard to die of dissipation before he was killed by his consumption. She had many other lovers, too, before, during, and after, among them possibly the Prince of Wales, though all she claimed about him was that he used to walk her dogs in the passage des Panoramas, at the back of the Variétés, while she was on. In *Hélène*, when she sang her number asking Venus what pleasure the goddess could find in making women's virtue *cascader*, the young bloods in the audience would call out 'Cascade, Hortense!' Like Vivette she was always giving up the stage – she was busy giving it up when Offenbach first tried to persuade her to sing Helen. Her furniture had already been packed up for removal back to Bordeaux, her home town, when he shouted his proposal through the letter-box of her locked front door. Fortunately a piano remained in the empty house, on which he played over the music to her – though finally persuading her also involved the offer of a lot more money. Like Vivette, too, she once refused at the last minute to appear on the first night of a new work (*La Grande-duchesse de Gerolstein*, because the censor had forbidden her to wear a prop royal order) and only relented when she heard the overture start.

Vivette's ignorance of the legend of Helen and Paris may seem far-fetched (or disingenuous), but no more so

than that of the *cocotte* who was famously said to have
refused to meet a friend because she was reading the
current best-seller, Renan's *La Vie de Jésus*, and was
desperate to find out how the story ended. Nor is the
supposed competition from Wagner quite as preposterous
as it seems – according to Faris, critics saw them as
rivals, and championed them against each other.
Offenbach wrote a parody of Wagner, and Wagner
never forgave him. The year before *Hélène*, a production
of *Tristan* in Vienna was cancelled in favour of a new
piece by Offenbach. All the same, in later life Wagner
said that Offenbach 'writes like the divine Mozart'.
Rossini, too, called him 'our little Mozart of the
Champs-Elysées'. Both were being a little over-generous,
perhaps, but a life of Mozart was Offenbach's bedside
book on all his travels, and Wagner and Rossini plainly
have a better ear for the music than Zola did.

I've compressed the time-scale of the decade. But in
1870 the Paris crowds did shout for war with Prussia –
they're out on the streets at the end of Zola's novel, as
Nana lies dying in a hotel bedroom, suppurating with
smallpox. The pretext for the war was almost as artificial
as the one in my version, and the man at the centre of
the crisis was the same. Within two months Paris was
besieged – and Gambetta, the new young Minister of
War, escaped to join other members of the Government
at Tours by precisely the same novel means of transport
as my heroes. But by that time the Emperor himself had
been captured at Sedan and the Second Empire had
collapsed – which really is the end of our story.

Meilhac and Halévy were right about the two Ajaxes
– in the *Iliad* Great and Little Ajax are close fighting
companions, even though their having the same name is
entirely coincidental. It was irresistible to transform them
into the Goncourt brothers, who were writing their
Journal all through these years in such close collaboration
that no one knows who wrote what. My representation
of them is as unfair as Meilhac and Halévy's was of

Menelaus, or Zola's of Schneider. They did hang around
theatres, though, trying to get their plays put on, and
they left a marvellous description of the backstage world
as they glimpsed it from the director's box at the Opéra
– evidently upstage of the curtain – one night in 1862.
Perhaps I could make some slight amends by letting
them have the last word and quoting it here; though
whether it's Edmond or Jules writing is as mysterious as
ever:

> While I make conversation, I have my eyes on the
> wings facing me. Holding on to a wooden upright, lit
> by the Argand lamp she is standing by, is la Mercier
> – very blonde, and very weighed down with gilt
> baubles and paste – radiant in a reddish light that
> brings out the smooth whiteness of her skin under the
> glitter of fake jewels. With one cheek and one
> shoulder kissed and flamed by the brilliance of the
> lamp, she is modelled like the girl with the chicken in
> Rembrandt's *Night Watch*. Then, behind the luminous
> figure of the dancer, a marvellous background of
> shadows and glimmerings, of darkness pricked by
> highlights, half-revealing, in smoky, dusty
> remotenesses, fantastic silhouettes of old women in
> battered hats, with bonnet-straps made of
> handkerchiefs around the lower parts of their faces,
> then overhead, on the walkways, like passengers
> dangling their legs through the rails of a ship, bodies
> – heads – overalls – of stagehands waiting attentively
> in monkey poses . . .
> The curtain falls, the rocks go down into the
> depths of the understage, the clouds go up into the
> flies, the blue heavens climb back behind the sky-
> pieces, the doors and windows are taken down and
> depart piece by piece into the wings, and bit by bit
> the bare core of the theatre appears. It is as if one
> were seeing all life's illusions departing one by one.
> Like these clouds, like this backcloth – so too do the
> horizons of our youth, our hopes, all our land of

dreams, gradually take wing into the skies. Like these rocks our great and lofty passions one by one sink and founder!

And these stagehands I see from my box on the stage, hurrying soundlessly in and out, bit by bit removing all these beautiful clouds and skies and landscapes, rolling up canvases and carpets – don't they represent the years, each one of which bears off in its arms some fine scene from our life, some peak it attained, some goblet made of wood, gilded wood, but which seemed gold to us?

And as I sat there lost in all this, my thoughts drifting, still looking at the completely bare and empty theatre, a voice from below called out: 'Inform those gentlemen in the stage-box.'

The opera had evidently ended. But why do operas end?

Characters

Vivette (*soprano*), *the great star of the Paris theatre*
M. Ploc (*tenor*), *a wealthy manufacturer, Vivette's protector*
The Baron (*baritone*), *banker of bankers, admirer of Vivette, investor in the theatre*
The Count (*tenor*), *member of the Jockey Club, admirer of Vivette, investor*
M. Edmond de Gonfleur (*tenor*), *a diarist*
M. Jules de Gonfleur (*tenor*), *another diarist, brother of the preceding*
M. Calcul (*bass*), *an impresario*
M. Berger (*tenor*), *a young man newly arrived in Paris from the provinces to seek his fortune*
Froufrou (*soprano*), *a cabaret entertainer*
Loulou (*soprano*), *likewise*
Zouzou (*soprano*), *likewise*
Marie (*mezzo*), *Vivette's maid*
M. Boulot (*silent*), *M. Calcul's secretary, stage manager, artistic adviser, financial director, public relations consultant, prompter, general understudy, etc.*
Signor A. Poggiatura (*tenor*), *in fact the most famous tenor in the world*
Investors, **Singers**, **Flowergirls**, **Waiters**, **Stagehands**, **Wardrobe Women**, **Theatregoers**, *etc.*

Setting   Paris in the 1860s

Note   Lyrics have been indented. Other lines are spoken – some of them to be spoken over underscoring.

La Belle Vivette was first presented by English National Opera at the Coliseum, London, on 11 December 1995, with the following cast:

Vivette	Lesley Garrett (some performances Janis Kelly)
M. Ploc	Ryland Davies
The Baron	Christopher Booth-Jones
The Count	Francis Egerton
M. Edmond de Gonfleur	Harry Nicoll
M. Jules de Gonfleur	John Graham-Hall
M. Calcul	Andrew Shore (one performance Gordon Sandison)
M. Berger	Neill Archer (some performances Thomas Randle)
Froufrou	Fiona Kimm
Loulou	Kate McCarney
Zouzou	Rosemary Ashe
Marie	Linda Ormiston
M. Boulot	Billie Brown
Signor A. Poggiatura	David Dyer

Directed by Ian Judge
Conducted by James Holmes (some performances Alex Ingram)
Designed by John Gunter
Costumes by Deirdre Clancy
Lighting by Nigel Levings
Choreographed by Lindsay Dolan

Adapted from *La Belle Hélène*, with music by Jacques Offenbach and libretto by Henri Meilhac and Ludovic Halévy.

Act One

During the overture the curtain goes up to reveal a Paris boulevard at night, with a crowd of **Theatregoers** *hurrying towards a theatre. They take their places, and on stage we see* **Vivette**, *performing the finale of a show,* Pif-Paf Paris! *The theatre revolves. Backstage, watching* **Vivette**, *are her protector,* **M. Ploc**, *and her admirers, the* **Baron**, *the* **Count**, *and the* **Gonfleur Brothers**, *together with* **Marie**, *her maid, and the* **Stagehands. Vivette** *takes her calls, and is congratulated by her supporters. Everyone begins the last night party.*

Sopranos
Down comes the final curtain on another show.

Tenors *and* **Basses**
The run is done, the time has come before you know!

Sopranos
Last night tonight!

Tenors *and* **Basses**
Can this be right?

Sopranos
You have a little farewell do.

Tenors
A drink or two.

Sopranos
Two – or three!

Tenors
They're free!

Basses
Have three – they're free!

Sopranos
You say this was the finest cast you ever knew.

Tenors *and* **Basses**
You swear you'll keep in touch – of course you never do.

Sopranos
And truth to tell . . .

Tenors *and* **Basses**
The run was hell!

Sopranos *and* **Tenors**
But now we're through!

Basses
Let's go before we cry!

Sopranos
Keep our mascara dry!

Tenors
Keep your mascara dry!

Basses
Keep your mascara dry!
We won't cry if we try!

Sopranos
Kiss kiss! Kiss kiss! Must fly!

Tenors *and* **Basses**
We'll miss all this! Bye bye!

All
Such fun! So sad! Bye bye!

Vivette *goes off on the arm of* **M. Ploc**, *followed by the* **Count**, *the* **Baron**, *the* **Gonfleur Brothers**, *and the rest of the cast of* Pif-Paf Paris! *The* **Stagehands** *turn off the gaslight.*

Sopranos
The stage is dark, the empty gods and boxes yawn.

Basses
Till cleaners in the dawn let in the light.

Tenors
> Until the cleaners open up the doors at dawn.

Sopranos
> And in the light . . .

Tenors
> The joys of night . . .

Basses
> Joys nightly die!

The **Stagehands** *open the scenery dock to the daylight.*

Sopranos
> Lie grey and faded and forlorn.

Tenors
> Lie grey and faded and forlorn.

Basses
> Faded and forlorn.

The **Stagehands** *start to strike the set and clear up. From among them come* **M. Calcul**, *a jaundiced impresario, and* **M. Boulot**, *a wretched put-upon little man, weighed down with props and costumes.*

Calcul
> Where are they now, where are they,
> The shows of yesteryear?
> Where is it now, where is it,
> The world we fashioned here?
>
> Just half a hundredweight of band-parts,
> Torn togas, cardboard crowns!
> Wheel it all away in handcarts.
> To play provincial towns.

Calcul *and* **Sopranos**
> Yes, into some dark warehouse . . .

Calcul *and* **All**
> Our dreams of last night go!

Calcul *and* **Boulot** *come out of the back of the theatre into the sunshine, and walk along the boulevard, past cafés and news kiosks and flower-stands.*

Calcul (*speaking*)   So what do we do, Monsieur Boulot? We start all over again! We go out on to the boulevard and we find another show for Vivette to sing! And if we don't find one? We starve!

They are joined by **Flowergirls**, **Milliners**, **Bakers**, **Waiters** *with breakfast trays*, **Newspaper-sellers**, **Postmen**, *etc.*

Sopranos
The sun is shining and today's another day!

Tenors *and* **Basses**
The air is fresh and sweet, and summer's on its way!

Sopranos
The month is May!

Tenors *and* **Basses**
Today's the day!

Sopranos
And we're in Paris, don't forget!

Tenors
We won't forget! Not that!

Sopranos
Think of that!

Basses
Remember that!

Sopranos
Along the boulevard go pretty midinettes!

Tenors *and* **Basses**
You sip a coffee and break open a baguette.

Sopranos
Maybe today . . .

Tenors *and* **Basses**
Will be your day!

Sopranos *and* **Tenors**
It may, it may!

Basses
Today may be your day!

Sopranos *and* **Tenors**
May be your lucky day!

Basses
May be your lucky day!
Your lucky, lucky day!

Sopranos
It may, it may, it may!

Tenors *and* **Basses**
Who knows, maybe today . . .

All
Will be your lucky day!

Sopranos
You buy a buttonhole – your hopes are riding high.

Basses
Days fine as this will surely never die!

Tenors
A day as fine as this will surely never die!

Sopranos
Today may run!

Tenors
May run and run!

Basses
It may, it may!

Sopranos
Maybe for ever has begun!

Tenors
Maybe for ever has begun!

Basses
Ever has begun!

Enter two **Delivery Boys** *with packages.*

First Delivery Boy (*speaking*)   Monsieur Calcul? The producer?

Calcul   What's all this? (*Sings:*)

They've started to compose 'em!
New operas by the score!
And yet one feels one knows 'em –
We've seen 'em all before!

More tales of kings weighed down by riches,
More courtesans and flirts,
More nice girls dressed up in breeches,
Pursued by boys in skirts.

Two Delivery Boys *and* **Sopranos**
Will these make our soprano . . .

Two Delivery Boys, **Sopranos**, **Tenors** *and* **Basses**
. . . Agree to sing once more?

Calcul (*speaking over music*)   Well, who knows? We'll go and try them on her.

Sopranos
So Paris goes upon its giddy, golden way.

Tenors *and* **Basses**
Whatever tune you want to dance to we can play!

Sopranos
If you can pay!

Tenors *and* **Basses**
We'll play away!

Sopranos
You want new hats? You want new shoes?
Pay and choose!

Tenors
If you can pay – you choose!

Basses
You pay and choose!

Sopranos
We've every kind of new and strange, exciting toys!

Basses
Strange, new, exciting toys when pleasure cloys!

Tenors
Such strange and new exciting toys when pleasure
cloys!

Sopranos
Bizarre new joys!

Tenors
There *are* new joys!

Basses
When old ones pall!

All
All sorts of games for girls and boys!

Wake up, enjoy today!
Enjoy it while you may!
Wake up, wake up, and play!
Wake up, wake up, and pay!
King yesterday is dead!
So long live King Today!

The interior of **Vivette**'s *house. Enter* **Marie**, *followed by*
Boulot, *who is carrying the pile of scores.*

Marie   More scores for Madame? More flowers?
Where am I to put them all? Over here . . . Over
there . . . Give them to me . . . Take them outside . . .

Boulot *begins to open the door. Cries of excitement from the*

Flowergirls *outside.*

Marie And tell those silly girls to leave their flowers and go. They'll wake Madame up with their chatter! And for heaven's sake . . .

Boulot *opens the door to go, and the* **Flowergirls** *come bursting in.*

Marie . . . don't let them in here!

First Flowergirl We want to see Mademoiselle Vivette!

Second Flowergirl Is it true she has a hundred dresses?

Third Flowergirl *Two* hundred dresses!

Fourth Flowergirl I heard a thousand!

First Flowergirl And live peacocks in her bedroom?

Second Flowergirl And Barbary apes?

Third Flowergirl And lovers?

Fourth Flowergirl And is terribly unhappy?

First Flowergirl There she is!

Vivette *appears on the landing above them* en déshabille. **M. Ploc** *appears behind her, holding some of the flowers that have just been delivered.*

Flowergirls
>Such an inspiration just to see her!
>Every girl in Paris wants to be her!
>Please God let a miracle occur:
>Let us be
>Loved like her
>By a wealthy manufacturer!

Vivette
>Yet only sad and empty-hearted
>Can I be,

For love my life has long departed.

If love must die,
Then so must we!

Flowergirls
Oh, so must we!

Vivette *comes slowly down the stairs.*

Vivette
No more, no more the secret glances,
That only two can understand;
The meetings made by sudden chances;
The passing touch of hand on hand.

How the longing lingers –
It haunts us, it taunts us.
For one sip of that sweetness
Our aching senses cry!
Love, before we die!
– One more taste of the honey!
Love, before we die!
Give us love or we die!

Women's Chorus
Love, before we die!
– One more taste of the honey!

Vivette
Love, before we die!
Give us love or we die!

No more, no more the stolen kisses,
The longed-for step outside the door,
The secret smile the dull world misses –
No more, no more, oh, never more!

How the longing lingers, *etc.*

Ploc   Come, come, my pet! Wandering about the
house with nothing on! The Baron will be here any
minute – the Count – all my friends in the business

world, on our way to the Stock Exchange! What *will*
they say?

Vivette   The Baron? The Count? I'll tell you what
they'll say. 'A signal from the window, my darling, as
soon as Monsieur Ploc is out of the house!'

Ploc   Off you go, my dear. Monsieur Calcul has
brought some new scores for you. Try to find some nice
new piece to keep you occupied.

The sounds of a march, off.

Marie   Here they come! The Baron! The Count! The
money!

The street outside. Enter the **Baron**, *the* **Count**, *and the*
Gonfleur Brothers. **Ploc** *joins them.*

Investors
Off to work
We gaily go!
Never shirk!
We love it so!

Stocks and shares
Are our delight.
Bulls and bears
Love us on sight.

Buy them low!
Up they go!
Who knows why?
Sell them high!

Cash, cash, cash, cash!

Grimy mills
Put francs in banks.
Shiny tills
Go clank with thanks.

Flash the cash,
We've won the pot!

Make a splash –
It's ours, why not?

Baron   Steel is strong!

Edmond de Gonfleur   What do you feel about
water?

Baron   Reasonably liquid.

Ploc   The coming thing is gas.

Baron   Gas? A flash in the pan.

Investors
Make a hash
When things get hot.
We go smash
And lose the lot!

Dash for cash
And buy like hell!
Others crash –
So all ends well!

Off to work!
Off to work!
Off we go!

Inside **Vivette**'s *house.* **Boulot** *is at the piano, waiting to
accompany* **Calcul***, who has a stack of scores in front of him.*
Vivette *is taking breakfast.*

Calcul   . . . And then, in Act Two, this wonderful duet.
Listen . . . Entirely new – arrived this morning.
Composed exclusively for you. In the style of Monsieur
Meyerbeer.

Vivette   I'm sick of Monsieur Meyerbeer.

Calcul   Of course. Yes. Listen . . . There stands
Clorinda.

He gives a copy of the score to **Marie***.*

Calcul (*to* **Vivette**)   This is you, Clorinda, you're

Clorinda . . . Moonlight. Shimmering strings . . . Sixteenth
century – low-cut dress . . . Beside you in the moonlight
stands Alphonse, the man to whom you have given your
heart.

Vivette   Monsieur Toupet?

Calcul   Or Monsieur Tisane, if you prefer. But what
you don't know is that Alphonse is one of the plotters
who have sworn revenge upon your family! Now . . .

Vivette   This is me?

Calcul   This is you. Andante amoroso.

Marie *sings* **Clorinda**, **Calcul** *sings* **Alphonse**.

Clorinda
Mine thou art!
Mine! Ah, mine!
Never to part!
I am thine!

Calcul   Alphonse . . .

(*As* **Alphonse**.)
No, no! It cannot be!
Our destiny is other.
For, alas, oh, woe is me!
I have to slay thy brother!

Clorinda
No, no, no!

Alphonse
Yes, oh, yes!

Clorinda
But why must this be so?

Alphonse
Explain my motivation I cannot.
But it is necessary for the plot.

Clorinda
Oh, not the plot!

Alphonse
Yes, the plot.

Clorinda
No, not the plot!

Alphonse
Yes, the plot.

Clorinda
That cursed plot! I had forgot!

Vivette   No.

Calcul   No?

Vivette   I'm sick of plots! I'm sick of playing characters called Clorinda!

Marie *discreetly goes out with the breakfast tray.*

Calcul   No matter. I have another score here. Also an entirely new work.

Vivette   In the style of Monsieur Meyerbeer?

Calcul   In the style of Signor Bellini.

Vivette   I'm sick of Signor Bellini! I'm giving up the stage!

Calcul   Of course you're giving up the stage! You give up the stage once a fortnight! You give it up very beautifully! We all want to see you give it up again and again! But how can you give it up again and again if we don't find another show for you to perform?

Music, off, and the sound of young women laughing and shouting.

Vivette   Now what ... ?

Enter **Marie**.

Marie   A troupe of entertainers, Madame. I told them

Madame was not at home.

Vivette   A troupe of entertainers?

Marie   Low entertainers, Madame. From a bar, or worse.

Vivette   *They're* not bringing me an opera to sing?

Marie   Yes, Madame.

A troupe of cabaret **Entertainers***, bursts in, laughing. Their leader is* **Froufrou***. Two of them,* **Loulou** *and* **Zouzou***, are propelling an innocent and handsome young man,* **M. Berger***.*

Vivette   I shall never leave my room again!

She sweeps away up the stairs and off.

Marie   I told you – she's not at home!

Froufrou   So we'll tell Monsieur Calcul!

Loulou (*to* **Calcul**)   Sit down!

Zouzou   Listen!

Froufrou
Me and the girls we're dancing the can-can
Down in a little cabaret.
In comes a fellow, starving composer,
Eats like a horse and then can't pay.

Loulou
What could we do?

Zouzou
Good-looking lad.

Froufrou
Me and the girls go all soft-hearted.

Calcul
Send for the police or you'll be had!
Fools and their money soon are parted.

Froufrou

What could we say? What could we do?

Chorus

What could we say? What could we do?

Calcul

You could say No! No, no, no, no!
You could say Go! Go, go, go, go!

Froufrou

Come on down!
Hit the town!
Table there for you,
At the Blue Cockatoo!

Place Pigalle –
Nice locale!
Come and have a few
At the Blue Cockatoo!

Everyone!
You'll have fun!
Here is what we do
At the Blue Cockatoo!

Entertainers, **Chorus**, **Calcul** *and* **Froufrou**

Skirts up high!
Why be shy?
Shake a lot of lace
In the customer's face!

Kick – two, three!
You might see
Just a little more
Than you bargained for!

One more flash
Then pay cash!
Get a better view
At the Blue Cockatoo!

Froufrou

Writes us a song instead of payment,

Writes us a song across the bill.
We must be crazy, what can you do, though?
Tuck it away inside the till.

Loulou
Next day he's back.

Zouzou
Starving again.

Froufrou
Steak and chips and writes another one.

Calcul
You must be simple, that's quite plain,
Soon you'll be feeding ev'ry mother's son.

Froufrou
What could we say? What could we do?

Chorus
What could we say? What could we do?

Calcul
You could say No! No, no, no, no!
You could say Go! Go, go, go, go!

Froufrou
Gilt saloons!
Clean spittoons!
Everything is new
At the Blue Cockatoo!

Bags of plush!
Loos that flush!
Cost a pretty sou
Did the Blue Cockatoo!

Plus plus plus –
Us us us!
Just along the rue
At the Blue Cockatoo!

Entertainers, **Chorus**, **Calcul** *and* **Froufrou**
Skirts up high! *etc.*

Froufrou
Now we've a till that's chock full of music
Jingle of coins is heard no more.
We've all the songs you need for an op'ra!
Make us an offer – buy the score.

Loulou
Must have the cash.

Zouzou
Go for a song.

Froufrou
You do the show – we'll all be in it.

Calcul
You've let yourselves be strung along.
Seems to be one born ev'ry minute.

Froufrou
What do you say? Say Yes you may!

Chorus
What do you say? Say Yes you may!

Calcul
I say No no! No, no, no, no!
I say Go go! Go, go. Go, go!

Froufrou
Bring a friend!
Set a trend!
Load up all the gang
In a big charabanc!

Bring your dad!
He's a lad!
Why not Uncle Jean
And your cousin from Toulon?

Wives as well!
What the hell!
If you're tired of yours
Try the man next door's!

Entertainers, **Chorus**, **Calcul** *and* **Froufrou**
Skirts up high! *etc.*

Calcul *tries to shepherd the* **Entertainers** *out.*

Calcul   Thank you. Thank you.

Calcul *indicates* **Boulot**. **Froufrou** *waves* **Berger**'s *score about under* **Calcul**'s *nose.*

Froufrou (*to* **Calcul**)   He's called Monsieur Berger!

Loulou   He's a country boy!

Zouzou   He's come to Paris to make his fortune!

Calcul   We'll put it with all the other scores. If we require a can-can in an opera at any point my staff will be in touch with you.

Calcul *shepherds them all towards the door.* **Vivette** *appears unnoticed at the head of the stairs and watches.*

Vivette   Wait!

Froufrou   It's her!

Vivette   This opera . . . It's not in the style of Monsieur Meyerbeer?

Calcul   No, no, no.

Vivette   Or Signor Bellini?

Calcul   It's not in any style at all. It's some ridiculous farrago he dreamed up himself.

Vivette   Who did?

Froufrou *and* **Others**   He did!

They push **Berger** *forward.* **Vivette** *comes slowly down the stairs, inspecting* **Berger**. *He gazes at her, overcome.*

Vivette You?

Froufrou *and* **Others** Yes!

They hold out the tattered manuscript.

Vivette You wrote it for me?

Froufrou *and* **Others** Yes!

Vivette And what's it about?

Loulou It all happens in ancient Greece ...

Zouzou He learnt about it at school ...

Vivette Can't he speak?

Froufrou *and* **Others** Tell her!

Berger It's about the most beautiful woman in the world.

Vivette The most beautiful woman in the world?

Berger Helen! Helen of Troy!

Vivette Let me see.

Berger *hands her the manuscript, and she looks through it.*

Calcul (*to* **Vivette**) It's not your style, my dear! (*To* **Berger**.) Quite wrong, I'm afraid!

Vivette This song, perhaps ...

The voice-line of the first verse of 'No more, no more', but played by an oboe or clarinet.

Berger You sing it one day when you're feeling sad.

Vivette But I know it!

Berger You know it?

Vivette I've always known it! Always and always!

Berger So where did you hear it?

Vivette Where ... ? Here! In my heart!

Berger   But the words . . .

Vivette   I know the words!

She puts the manuscript in front of **Boulot**. **Boulot** *puts his hands on the piano, but what emerges this time is the full orchestral accompaniment.*

Vivette
How the longing lingers
It haunts us, it taunts us.
For one sip of that sweetness
Our aching senses cry!
Love, before we die!
– One more taste of the honey!
Love, before we die!
Give us love or we die!

Entertainers
Love, before we die!
– One more taste of the honey!

Vivette
Love, before we die!
Give us love or we die!

(*Speaking.*) And so I'm the most beautiful woman in the world?

Berger   Yes! And you're married to the richest man in the world, and you live in the most beautiful palace in the world, and all the most famous men in the world are in love with you!

Vivette   And still I'm not happy?

Berger   And still you're not happy. Until one day . . .

Vivette   Yes?

Berger   A young man arrives . . .

Vivette   A handsome young man?

Berger   The most handsome man in the world.

Vivette   And they fall in love with each other?

Berger   They can't help themselves!

Vivette   Really?

Berger   No, because they're fated! Because he was promised her by Venus, the goddess of love!

Vivette   And why did Venus do that?

Berger   Because of what happened with the apple. You don't know about the apple?

He takes an apple from a bowl.

When the handsomest man in the world was out walking one day in the countryside? And he came face-to-face with these three great goddesses?

He puts his manuscript in front of **Boulot**, *and brings forward* **Froufrou**, **Loulou** *and* **Zouzou**.

Berger   Imagine these are the three goddesses.

Vivette   What about the most handsome man in the world?

Berger   We'll come to him. (*Sings:*)

In ancient times one day three goddesses
Began to disagree.
'Who is the most divinely beautiful,'
They argued, 'of us three?'

And weigh heigh! All these great goddesses,
They know a trick or two!
Oh, weigh heigh! Tricks to get round poor boys,
They do, my word, they do,
Oh my word, yes, my word, but they do, they do!

Now a simple shepherd lad came by,
All piping innocently (like me!).
For his lunch he held an apple,
As idyllic as can be.

'Oh . . . !
Simple young man, we need your apple
For a scientific test.
Pray just hand it to whichever one
You like the look of best.'

Oh, weigh heigh! But they have tricks to play,
They do, my word, they do!
Oh, weigh heigh! Tricks to get round poor boys,
They do, my word, they do,
Oh my word, yes, my word, but they do, they do!

Loulou *approaches.*

Berger
 Said the first: 'If taste and culture count
 Then I'm the one you seek.
 I've degrees in Jurisprudence,
 Like to cook, speak fluent Greek.'

 And weigh heigh! These famous goddesses,
 They know a trick or two . . . !

Loulou *is replaceed by* **Zouzou**.

Berger
 Said the second: 'Helping people is my dearest aim in
  life.
 Saving furry animals and settling international strife.'

 But weigh heigh! They know devices,
 Yes, some most intriguing tricks –
 Oh, they do, my word, they do!

 But the third, oh, the third said nothing –
 Not a syllable said she.
 But it was she who got the apple . . .

He takes a bite out of the apple and gives it to **Froufrou***, who looks boldly at him and takes a bite out of it in her turn.*

Berger
 And now words are failing me!

Oh, weigh heigh! All these great goddesses,
They know a trick or two!
Oh, weigh heigh! Tricks to get round poor boys,
They do, my word, they do!
My word, my word, but they do!

Loulou *and* **Zouzou** *turn upon* **Froufrou**, *who runs to hide her confusion.*

Vivette (*to* **Calcul**)   Perhaps we should begin to think about a comeback . . .

Calcul   Of course. Excellent, excellent. But not with *this*, my dear! The boy is unknown! Where would I find the money?

Froufrou   Your investors!

Zouzou   The Baron! The Count!

Loulou   Monsieur Ploc!

Calcul   I'm sorry. But times are hard. The stock market is very uncertain . . .

Froufrou   Listen!

A restaurant, full of excited **Parisians**. *Enter the* **Investors**.

Parisians
Home come the heroes back from war!
With battle-honours by the score!
From the Stock Exchange!
Kings who rule the trading floor!

They've done it once again!
They're winners!
Break out the good champagne,
Give dinners!

Home come the heroes back from war! *etc.*

Hurrah, hurrah
For all our jobbers and brokers!
Hurrah, hurrah
For all their hocus-pocus!

Hurrah, hurrah, hurrah, hurrah, hurrah!

Froufrou   So, Monsieur Ploc, what happened at the
Stock Exchange?

Loulou *and* **Zouzou**   Tell us! Tell us!

Ploc
I sold gold. Went into cocoa, deep into cocoa, lapped
   up the cocoa.
Cornered quite a block!

Others
Oh, well done, Monsieur Ploc!

Ploc
I buy rye. Start with a little, hardly a tittle, merely *un
   poco*.
Cocoa takes a knock!

Others
So what now, Monsieur Ploc?

Ploc
I collar the dollar market, steady as a rock.
I hold gold. Get out of cocoa, right out of cocoa,
   cocoa's a joke! Oh,
Gave them all a shock or else my name's not Ploc.

Others
He sold gold, went into cocoa, deep into cocoa.
   Cornered quite a block!
He held gold, got out of cocoa, right out of cocoa!
Typical of Ploc!

Froufrou   And, Monsieur le Comte, what did *you* do?

Loulou *and* **Zouzou**   Tell us! Tell us!

Count
A count can't seem to be counting, vulgarly counting,
   commonly counting
Mercenary gains.

Others
> There's blue blood in his veins!

Count
> One can't count sordid accounting, wretched
>   accounting, lowly accounting,
> Fit for noble brains.

Others
> She mustn't strain his brains!

Count
> A duel or two to do is all that blue blood deigns.
> A count counts on his accountants, loyal accountants
>   – long live accountants! – making all his gains
> Without unseemly pains.

Others
> A count can't seem to be counting, vulgarly counting,
> Mercenary gains!
> A count counts on his accountants, loyal accountants,
> Saving all his pains!

Froufrou   And what did the Gonfleur Brothers do?

Loulou   Tell us!

Zouzou   Tell us!

Both Gonfleurs
> We two . . .

Edmond de Gonfleur
> . . . who . . .

Jules de Gonfleur
> . . . write every day to-

Edmond
> . . . gether, and play to-

Jules
> . . . gether all day, too –

Both Gonfleurs
We always concur!

Others
You know the Frères Gonfleur?

Both Gonfleurs
We do . . .

Edmond
    . . . – true! –

Jules
    . . . both know the way to . . .

Edmond
      . . . say who today who . . .

Jules
      . . . knows what we may do.

Both Gonfleurs
No need to confer!

Others
The famous Frères Gonfleur!

Edmond
We'll tell you . . .

Jules
    . . . the company . . .

Edmond
      . . . whose shares . . .

Both Gonfleurs
      . . . we both prefer.

Jules
So *you* say.

Edmond
No, brother – *you*, pray!

Jules
> Your turn, so do say!

Edmond
> Why don't we two say?

Both Gonfleurs
Our own private company – the Frères Gonfleur!

Others
These two do know who can say who may say today
who
Knows what they may do!
It's just as well seeing no one else has a clue
Which one of them is who!

Froufrou   And Monsieur le Baron!

Loulou   Banker of bankers!

Zouzou   What did the bank do?

Baron
You ask me: What did the bank do, what could the
bank do, what should the bank do,
On this famous day?

Others
Oh, tell us, Baron, pray!

Baron
So glad you asked me! I thank you, first let me thank
you, frankly I thank you,
In this humble way.

Others
Now, please, no more delay!

Baron
I'll tell you our policy quite plainly, if I may.
Since I'm head man of the bank, who, man of the
bank, who, man of the bank, who
Better to explain we never, ever say?

Others

We ask him: what did the bank do, what did the
bank do,
On this famous day?
He will not say what the bank did, say what the bank
did,
On this famous day!

The five great men all congratulate each other.

Parisians

Home go the heroes back from war!
With battle-honours by the score!
From the Stock Exchange!
The Stock Exchange!
Kings who rule the trading floor!

Hurrah, Hurrah
For all our jobbers and brokers!
Hurrah, hurrah
For all their hocus-pocus!

Hurrah, hurrah, hurrah, hurrah, hurrah!

The **Investors** *and* **Entertainers** *arrive in* **Vivette**'s
salon, where **Vivette**, **Calcul**, **Boulot**, *and* **Marie** *are
waiting.*

Ploc   So has my little songbird found a new song for
us? She was giving up the stage when I left the house
this morning!

Both Gonfleurs   Again!

Baron   What – the darling of Paris? The toast of the
town?

Count   You'll break our hearts!

Edmond   And you've broken them . . .

Jules   . . . so many times already!

Ploc   So, Monsieur Calcul, what have you found for
her?

Calcul   A most charming piece in the style of Monsieur Meyerbeer . . .

Froufrou   They've found *this*.

Ploc   This?

Calcul   Mademoiselle Vivette was kind enough to take an interest in it, but . . .

Froufrou   It's by Monsieur Berger.

Loulou   He's from the country!

Froufrou   We're all going to be in it!

Zouzou   All we need is the money to put it on!

Ploc   Money? Yes, well, money is hard to come by these days.

Baron   A national need for financial discipline . . .

Count   Retrenchment . . .

Edmond   Soaring costs . . .

Jules   Credit restrictions . . .

Froufrou (*to* **Berger**)   Tell them what it's about.

Berger   It's about . . . It's about the most beautiful woman in the world.

Ploc   The most beautiful woman in the world?

Berger   And although she is the most beautiful woman in the world, she is very sad, because she feels that love has passed her by. And then one day . . .

Ploc   A handsome young man arrives.

Berger   The most handsome man in the world.

Ploc (*smoothes his beard*)   Ah!

Baron   Really?

Count   Well, dash me!

Berger   And they know that fate has destined them for each other.

Ploc, **Baron**, **Count**, **Both Gonfleurs** (*aside, simultaneously*)   Our story!

Ploc   One is of course always looking for an interesting new investment.

Calcul   Oh, it's a very fine score, Monsieur Ploc. And if the markets are currently buoyant . . .

Baron   We all need a placement for short-term funds.

Edmond   And if we can give some encouragement to the arts . . .

Jules   In reasonable safety . . .

Count   Let's take a squint . . . By God! All these Greek fellows! Met them somewhere before!

Ploc   Met them before?

Both Gonfleurs   Where? Where?

Baron   I don't believe I'm acquainted with any Greeks.

Both Gonfleurs   No, but they're just like us!

Ploc   Like us?

Count   Listen! (*Sings:*)

Here's me, hotblooded Achilles, temper like chillis,
    raging Achilles,
Famous man of steel!

Others
The fellow with the heel!

Both Gonfleurs
Here's two . . .

Edmond
. . . Kings . . .

Jules
> . . . both with the same aim . . .

Edmond
> . . . both in the fame game . . .

Jules
> . . . both with the same name . . .

Both Gonfleurs
> . . . Ajax One and Two.

Calcul *and* **Froufrou**
> These two are just like you!

Count
> By God, I can feel a tender tendon in my heel!

Both Gonfleurs
> And yes, he's pictured us neatly, rather discreetly,
> perfectly sweetly!

Count *and* **Both Gonfleurs**
> This man understands completely
> How we feel!

Baron
> So I must be Agamemnon, King Agamemnon, great
> Agamemnon!
> King of Kings, you see!

Others
> You surely must be he!

Ploc
> And here's me! King Menelaus! See – Menelaus! Me
> – Menelaus!
> Husband of the queen!

Others
> Fair Helen is his queen.

Baron
> And that gives us all a sporting chance without a
> doubt!

Ploc
Our two hearts perfectly blending!
Nice happy ending
Clearly impending!

Baron *and* **Ploc**
Here's a man who plainly knows us
inside out!

Others
It's true that even a hero's more like a hero
dignified by art.
And maybe even a zero's less like a zero in a hero's
part!
So here's to art! So here's to art!

Edmond (*speaking*)   But this is exactly what we have
been calling for!

Jules   An opera relevant to the society we live in!

Baron   The work must be performed!

Calcul   We'll start rehearsals tomorrow!

Vivette   Have you forgotten? I'm giving up the stage!

Calcul   She's giving up the stage!

Baron (*to* **Vivette**)   Change your mind! We all implore
you!

Count   Do it for our sake, Vivette!

Both Gonfleurs   Do it for the sake of art!

Calcul   Do it for the money!

Ploc   She'll do it if I ask her. (*Pause.*) Won't you?

Froufrou   I know what she'll do it for! She'll do it for
all the people of this town! The town where she was
born! The town she's toast of! She'll do it for Paris!

All *except* **Vivette** *and* **Berger**   Yes! For Paris! Do it for
Paris! (*Sing.*)

Paris! Paris!
Magic is in the very name!
Song after song proclaims its fame!
Paris, ah, Paris!
You can't resist that name!

Berger

The name,
If this be true,
Makes my claim
Twice as strong!
For the man in my song
His name is Paris, too!

All *except* **Berger** *and* **Vivette**

Ah ha!

Vivette

He's Paris? What, Paris? Like Paris,
My own dear Paris?
My lovely Paris?

Berger

Your own dear Paris, yes!

Others

Paris! The town you're the toast of!
The town you're the boast of!

Vivette

Ah, my Paris!

Others

How you love . . .

Vivette *and* **Others**

. . . that name!

Vivette

That name I love so dearly!
I feel so nearly!
Sounding so clearly!
It runs with sunshine,
It sings of springtime!

Others

Fate!

Vivette

It brings back soft summer nights,
Forgotten winter delights!
The places my heart has sighed over,
Laughed, yes, and cried over!
My life and love!
So fate has plainly spoken.
My will has broken.
What can my answer be?

Others

What can her answer be?

Vivette

If Paris wants me I agree!

Others

What can she do but agree!

Ploc

And all at once your eyes are brighter,
Your cheeks are flushed, your step is lighter.
Your heart – it feels alive,
And all your senses revive!
Unless I'm wildly wrong,
My lovebird's back on song!
She is right back on song!
So you agree to play, dear?

Vivette

Yes! Anything you say, dear.

M. Ploc *shakes* **Berger**'s *hand.*

Others

Here's the news we're all waiting for!
Our Vivette is singing once more!
Here's the news we're all waiting for!
Our Vivette will sing once more!

Ploc
> To seal the deal, we'll take a glass of punch.
> (*To* **Berger**.) I trust that you've no great objection
> If we talk money over lunch?

Vivette (*to* **M. Ploc**)
> I don't lunch, as you know, dear.
> But this time I will make an exception.

Berger
> There's just one tricky little matter to be settled first:
> She will be she, but, tell me, who'll be he?

Vivette
> Yes, who will sing with me?
> Who can my tenor be?

Calcul (*aside, to* **Berger**)
> You mean it should be you?

Berger (*aside, to* **Calcul**)
> If Monsieur Ploc were not nearby
> I'd be prepared to have a try.
> Duets for three are hard to do –
> All my duets are songs for two.

Calcul
> So that's the quid pro quo!

Berger
> Think how to make him go.

Calcul
> Rack your brains, Monsieur Boulot!

Baron
> Sub-committee report:
> Tell the board just how we ought
> To proceed
> With all due speed
> To fill a post of that sort.

Others
> Sub-committee report:
> Tell the board how we ought
> To proceed
> With all due speed
> To fill a post of that sort.

Boulot *steps forward to make his report. But* **Calcul** *forestalls him.*

Calcul
> A blinding flash of inspiration!
> I know what it is we must do
> To produce an almighty sensation!

Chorus
> He's thought it through!

Others
> Here's what we do!

Calcul
> Now, Monsieur Ploc.

Ploc
> Yes?

Calcul
> Search Europe near and far!
> Find a great opera star!
> Get the biggest and best!
> So, straight upstairs and pack!
> No need to hurry back!
> Time must not count in such a mighty quest!

Ploc
> This requires contemplation.

Vivette
> Go, go, you need a vacation.

Berger (*to* **Calcul**)
> Leave us to manage things at home.

Ploc
I don't feel any great temptation.

Count
Off you go on your vacation!

Vivette
Quick, off you go!

Baron *and* **Calcul**
To a distant destination!

Count *and* **Both Gonfleurs**
Off you go on your vacation!

Berger
Quick, off you go!

Baron *and* **Calcul**
On a very long vacation!

Vivette
Away you go!

Count, **Both Gonfleurs**, *and* **Basses**
A long vacation!

Berger
Away you go!

Baron, **Calcul**, **Tenors** *and* **Basses**
A long vacation!

Vivette, **Froufrou**, **Loulou** *and* **Zouzou**
Away, you go!
Away, away! Away! Away!

Ploc
I'm off on my vacation!

Chorus
Away you go! Away you go!
Away, away! Away! Away!

Vivette
But don't ask us where!

We don't really care!
So . . .
Have fun! Don't miss Majorca, Moscow or Malta,
    Minsk or Minorca!
Do see Genoa!

Others
And why not try Accra?

Vivette
So take care, don't drink the water, do tip the porter,
    never resort to
Strange girls in a bar!

Others
Especially in Accra!

Vivette
And send us a card, my precious – tell us how you
    are.
But please, please, don't cut it short, dear,
Do what you ought, dear,
Keep me in thought, dear –
You know how the heart grows fonder from afar.

Vivette *and* **Others**
So have fun. Don't miss Majorca, Moscow or Malta.
Do see Genoa!
So take care, don't drink the water, never resort to
Strange girls in a bar!

All
Away! Away! Away!
Go, go, go!

Berger *and* **Others**
Off to the station! Off to the station!

Berger
Off to the station!
Go, go, go!
Off to the station!

No more meditation!

Others
Go, go, go, go!
Take a long vacation! Go, go!

Vivette *and* **Berger**
Take a vacation!
No more hesitation! Go, go, go!

All
Go! Go! Take a vacation!

Ploc *boards a train and sets out on his travels.*

Vivette *and* **Others**
Play the noble part
Fate for you decrees,
Go for love of art
Over stormy seas!

Curtain.

Act Two

Backstage, in **Vivette***'s dressing-room.* **Vivette**, **Marie**, *and the* **Wardrobe Women**.

Marie Madame must wear *something*! The show opens next week! Madame is not going on stark naked?

Marie *and* **Wardrobe Women**
A world-famous queen must express
Her world-famous beauty
With a famous dress!

Everyone in Paris longs to know
To quite what lengths you'll dare to go.
To what outrageous lengths you'll go.

Marie
So wear too much, or else too little.

Vivette
No, no! No, no! No scandal or vulgar sensation!
Ploc is away. Poor Ploc is not yet back!
I mean to resist all temptation,
And turn to devout contemplation,
Dressed like a nun from head to foot in black.
Dressed like a nun from head to foot in black.

Marie
You could wear gold, or puce, or crimson,
Or shocking pink, with sky-blue trims on –
But not black!

Wardrobe Women
No, not black!

Marie *and* **Wardrobe Women**
No! No! No!
A world-famous queen must express, *etc.*
Oh, please – you've gone to such outrageous lengths before!
We long to see you go to more!

So show us less, or much, much more!

Marie *signals to the* **Wardrobe Women** *that they should leave.*

Marie I don't know what's the matter with Madame! You send Monsieur off on a wild goose chase . . .

Vivette It was just a game! I didn't really mean him to go!

Marie Now there he is, safely out of the way in Constantinople with digestive troubles . . .

Vivette Oh, Marie, what have I done? He'll die, he'll die!

Marie Now here's this one, waiting all morning for Madame to rehearse with him, and Madame won't even speak to him!

Vivette I'm frightened, Marie!

Marie The house? It's in Madame's name!

Vivette I didn't mean that!

Marie The jewels? The carriage? Madame, he's in Constantinople! He can't stir three metres from a water-closet!

Vivette No, no, no! Help me, Marie, or I may do something foolish!

Marie When has Madame ever been frightened of doing something foolish?

Berger *enters, holding sheets of music, and stands waiting humbly.* **Vivette** *sees him, but looks away.*

Vivette (*to* **Marie**) But never anything as foolish as the foolish thing I might do now!

Marie One last sip of the honey! That's what Madame wanted!

Vivette   A sip, Marie! Not a bath of it! To taste it,
Marie! Not to drown in it!

Marie   He's been waiting all morning, my precious!

Vivette   He's been waiting all night, outside my
window!

Marie   He can't wait for ever, poor soul!

Vivette   Send him away . . . No! Tell him . . . Tell him
I'm not dressed!

Marie   When did Madame start getting dressed before
she received a gentleman?

Berger   Marie . . . !

Marie   Not now, Monsieur.

Berger   But I've written a new song! It's for Vivette
and me to sing together!

Marie   She's not dressed, Monsieur.

Berger   I'll keep my eyes shut.

Marie   Later, Monsieur. Later. Leave it to me . . .

She takes **Berger** *out.*

Vivette
Some like to call me an enchantress –
The Queen of Love and all its arts.
They say that I have magic powers
To weave my spells around men's hearts.

And yet one heart can still deny me,
One heart alone remains unknown,
One heart continues to defy me;
And that one heart – it is my own!
Yes, that one heart – it is my own!

The nights grow cold. We light one little fire.
Now here's the hearth all ablaze, all ablaze, burning
   bright.

The flames grow bold. They leap up, ever higher!
Now here's the house all ablaze, all ablaze, in the
   night!

My heart longs only to be faithful,
Seeks only harmony and peace.
And, after all the storms and passion,
Sincerely yearns for strife to cease.

And yet this heart of mine is lying!
Because of one thing I am sure:
Although for peace I hear it sighing,
This rebel heart prepares for war!
My rebel heart prepares for war!

The nights grow cold. *etc.*

It's not my fault if men pursue me –
You see how hard I try to cope,
To hold them off yet not discourage,
To leave them all a breath of hope.

But if my heart will not obey me,
How can I manage to be true?
Yes, if my heart itself betray me,
How can I win? What can I do?
I must give in, and see it through!

The nights grow cold. *etc.*

Marie *enters, holding up more dresses.*

Vivette   And, Marie, if Monsieur Berger comes back,
tell him . . . Tell him I'm not going to sing with him.
Not now – not next week – not ever. I've made up my
mind, Marie! Do you understand? But the new song . . .
Oh, Marie, I wish I'd heard it first!

The voice of **Berger** *can be heard singing very softly,
unaccompanied, somewhere in the theatre.* **Vivette** *and* **Marie**
*gaze up into the galleries and gantries, trying to see where the
sound is coming from.*

Berger's voice
Everywhere,
In the air,
Something stirs. Is it here in my heart?
Is it there
In the air?

Vivette (*speaking*)   It's his song!

Bergers' voice
Or the light?

Vivette   Where is he?

Berger's voice
Like a voice from the past,
Or the sweet scent of night.

The orchestral accompaniment begins, very softly.

Vivette   I'm not listening!

Berger's voice   It's only a rehearsal (*Sings:*)

A song!

Vivette (*sings*)
A song!

Berger's voice
Just music!

Both
Ah!

Marie *reveals herself to be* **Berger** *in disguise. He runs towards* **Vivette**, *and they embrace. A noise of cheerful shouting, off.*

Vivette   Listen! Someone next door!

Berger   It's Monsieur Calcul! He's having a meeting today with all his investors!

The music starts. **Vivette** *drops the score and flees.* **Berger** *runs off after her.*

Berger   Vivette!

The boardroom of the theatre. **Calcul**, **Boulot** *and the*
Investors. **Boulot** *pours them all champagne.*

Investors
Cash to burn,
Hip, hip, hurrah!
So we turn
To opera!

Evening dress,
And large cigars.
Meet the press
And kiss the stars.

We invest
In the best!
Why not art?
Rather smart!

Chic chic chic chic!

Rows of seats
All needing bums.
Oh, the treats
For business chums!

Take a box
And have a do –
Lots of chocs
To see you through.

Vivette *enters and tries to talk privately to* **Calcul**.

Vivette   I'm not doing the show! I'm going abroad!

Calcul   Of course. Wonderful. Tell my personnel
manager tomorrow.

He indicates **Boulot**.

Vivette   By tomorrow I shall be a thousand miles
away . . .

Investors
Tra-la-li!
Must be good stuff –
Do re mi!
It cost enough!

Vivette *goes out.*

Investors
Life is short
And art is long –
Crafty snort
If things go on.
Opera!

Baron   Order, order . . . ! Thank you. One: minutes of the last meeting . . . ?

Murmurs of assent.

Two: apologies for absence . . . ?

Calcul   From Monsieur Ploc, in Constantinople – unavoidably detained in the fever hospital.

Baron   Telegram of sympathy on behalf of all his fellow-investors.

All   Hear, hear!

Baron   Three: your managing director's report on the year's trading. Monsieur Calcul . . .

Calcul   Thank you, thank you. I have two very exciting new developments to report. The first is that the Board has authorised the issue of another glass of free champagne!

Fanfare. The **Investors** *cheer.* **Boulot** *hastens to refill everyone's glass.*

Calcul   And the second piece of exciting news is that the Board has commissioned a projection of current trends in the leisure services market! And here to present

it, will you please welcome ... Mademoiselle Froufrou,
and the girls of the Blue Cockatoo!

Enter **Froufrou**, **Loulou**, **Zouzou** *and the other*
Entertainers. *Applause from the* **Investors**.

Froufrou
Here's to all our success tomorrow!
Drink to it now!

Entertainers
Toast it today!

Froufrou
Just in case it all ends in sorrow –
Celebrate first!

Entertainers
Come then what may!

Froufrou
Raise your glass and see the bubbles!
Soon each bubble will have burst.
Since we, too, may have our troubles –
Hold our celebration first!

All
La-la la-la la!

Froufrou *and the* **Entertainers** *sit down in the*
Investors' *laps, put their arms round them, refill their glasses.*

Baron   Thank you. Any other business? No other
business. In that case it only remains to settle the date
of the next meeting ...

Count   Wait! Some damn thing we've forgotten! What
is it?

Edmond   The dividend!

Jules   The dividend!

Edmond   What's the dividend!

Baron   Oh, yes, the dividend!

Investors   The dividend!

They all look towards **Calcul**.

Calcul   The dividend?

Investors   The dividend!

Calcul   Yes, well, the dividend . . . (*Sings:*)

> For that you'll have to wait.

Investors
> Wait?

Calcul
> We're not playing roulette! We've a solid investment!

Baron
> You don't mean that the rest went?
> Our holdings up to date?

Calcul
> Our new show! Once it's on . . .

Baron
> I do believe we've lost the lot!

Both Gonfleurs
> Yes, every penny that we've got!

Count
> But big returns were guaranteed!

Calcul
> Just one success – that's all we need!

Froufrou
> Us girls have all rehearsed our dance!

Loulou *and* **Zouzou**
> It's where we show our legs! The opera's our big
> chance!

Calcul
> Have faith in me – I've got the knack!

Investors

No, no, we want our money back!

Calcul

But you know me – you'll get your whack!

Investors

No, no, we want our money back!
We want it now – our money back!

Calcul

But I cannot
Pay on the dot!
Can't give you what
I haven't got!

Investors

Cash on the spot!
All you have got!
Pay out the pot!
Give us the lot!

Calcul

Don't care a lot
If you all rot!
Is it a plot
You've laid, or what?

Investors

Cash on the spot! *etc.*

Calcul

Oh, you forgot
That I said not?

Investors

Give us the lot! Give us the lot!

Calcul

No, not a jot!
So off you trot!

Both Gonfleurs

With due solemnity we warn you
That we will put you in our book.

Polite society will scorn you
When it sees how we make you look!

Investors
Give us the lot! Give us the lot!

Calcul
But I cannot *etc.*

Investors
Cash on the spot! *etc.*

The **Investors** *advance threateningly upon* **Calcul**. **Boulot**
picks up as many bottles of champagne as he can carry as they
flee.

Backstage. **Vivette**, *now fully dressed, and* **Marie**.

Vivette (*to* **Marie**)   Pack my bags, Marie! Buy tickets
for the train! You'll come with me, of course. And,
Marie – you may travel second-class.

Marie   Thank you, Madame. Where to, Madame?

Vivette   To Constantinople!

Marie   To Constantinople? But the show, Madame!
And Monsieur Berger!

Vivette   I'm giving up the stage, Marie!

Marie   Oh, yes. And shall I telegraph for rooms,
Madame?

Vivette   No, Marie. We shall be staying in the fever
hospital.

Vivette *hurries* **Marie** *out, then finds the sheets of music that*
Berger *gave her earlier.*

Vivette
Everywhere,
In the air,
Something stirs. Is it here in my heart?
Is it there
In the air?

Or the light?
Like a voice from the past.
Or the sweet scent of night.
Could it be music?

Berger (*from somewhere in the darkness*)
Echoes of music.

Vivette
Of music?

Berger
Of music.

Vivette
Of music!

Berger
Of music!

Berger *emerges from the darkness.*

Both
Ah!

Berger
Two people singing . . .

Vivette
Two people singing . . .

Both
Singing a sweet and simple song.

Berger
Lovers have sung it . . .

Vivette
Lovers have sung it . . .

Both
Since the world was young.

Vivette
Soon the notes fade . . .

Berger
Soon the notes fade . . .

Both
Soon the notes fade, and life moves on!

Berger
Sing it!

Vivette
Sing it!

Berger
Sing it!

Vivette
Sing it!
And sing till the song has been sung.

Berger
And sing till the song has been sung.
Ah!

Both
Ah!

Marie *enters, dressed for travel, carrying suitcases. She stops at the sight of them. They do not see her.*

Vivette
A song, a song, an old, sweet song!

Berger
A song, a song, an old, old sweet song!

Vivette
A song, a song, an old, sweet song!

Berger
A song, a song, an old, old sweet song!

Vivette
Two people singing!

Berger
Two people singing!

Both
Singing a sweet and simple song!

Berger
Two people singing!

Vivette
Two people singing!

Both
Singing a sweet, simple song – just . . . a song!

Marie *puts the suitcases down resignedly, takes off her hat, and goes out.*

Vivette
If this is just . . . a song,
And we are free to sing
All the things we never say.
I want to ask one thing . . .

Berger
It's a song. Ask me! Ask me! Ask away!

Vivette
You sang a different song . . . that day.
You said you loved another!

Berger
Never!

Vivette
Yes, in your song there was a girl who ate the apple.

Berger
Oh, Venus.

Vivette
Am I as beautiful, as beautiful as Venus?

Berger
As Venus?
I beg you to try and forget her;

It's only a song where I met her!
Though it's true . . .
I saw her . . .
From a lot closer to.

Vivette
How close was she?

Berger
Closer!

Vivette
Than me?

Berger
Two arms had mysteriously bound us!
Her golden hair tumbled around us!
So closely no one could have found us!
To keep my head quite clear
Was hard for me, I fear!

Vivette
Since this is just a song . . .

Berger
Only a passing song . . .

Vivette
Only an old, sweet song,
Is it wrong
If we . . . sing on?

Berger
Two people singing . . .

Vivette
Two people singing . . . *etc*.

So now! Now you can tell!

Berger
Vivette, Vivette, you're beautiful!
And yet, well . . .

Vivette

Well, what?

Berger

The appearance of Venus made its mark
On me so strongly because ... well ... well ...
We were in the dark!

Vivette

So the darkness helped you see?

Berger

Yes!

Vivette

More plain than you see me?

Berger

Yes! My two poor eyes were blind –
By touch I did the test.
So all these ten examiners
Questioned her for me!
Went roaming, roaming, free!
Nights in Greece are sultry –
Languid and sultry –
So that she was quite ...
Lightly dressed.

Vivette

Lightly dressed?

Berger

Lightly dressed!
To make a fair comparison
Here's what I'd suggest:
We find a similar darkness,
And we do a similar test!

Vivette

Since this is just a song ...

Berger

Only a passing song ...

Vivette

Only an old, sweet song,
Is it wrong
If we . . . sing on?

They move towards her dressing-room.

Berger

Two people singing . . .

Vivette

Two people singing . . . *etc.*

Both

Singing a sweet, simple song – just . . . a song!
We'll sing our song!
Oh, while we have breath to sing,
We'll sing, we'll sing our song!

They sink down on to the bed. **Ploc** *enters.*

Ploc   I'm back!

Vivette   But what are you doing here?

Ploc   What am *I* doing here? What are *you* doing here!

Berger   Welcome home, Monsieur.

Ploc   Please! Don't get up!

Vivette   We thought you were in Constantinople!

Ploc   So I observe.

Vivette   You surely don't imagine . . . ?

Ploc   I don't need to imagine!

Berger   We were merely rehearsing.

Ploc *rushes out of the dressing-room and back on to the stage.*

Ploc (*calls*)   Monsieur Calcul!

Vivette *and* **Berger** *follow him.*

Vivette   Wait! Wait!

Berger We were rehearsing!

Ploc (*calls*) Calcul! What's been going on here? (*Sings:*)

I'll sue! I'll call the Vice Squad! Calcul!

Vivette
You want the Vice Squad? What, to arrest us?

Berger
You want to scare off the investors?

Vivette
Rehearse! Rehearse! That's all we did! Rehearse!

Berger
Rehearse!

Ploc
Oh, is that right? And can we all reserve our seats for
your first night?

They run through the boardroom, where the **Investors** *and*
Entertainers *are now getting down to serious business together.*

Froufrou
Oh, a well-oiled wheel runs easy.
Oil the wheels!

Investors
Oil the wheels!

Froufrou
So let's get all our bearings greasy!
How good it feels!

Investors
Turning like wheels!

Froufrou
Raise your glass and see the bubbles!
Soon each bubble will have burst!
Since we, too, may have our troubles –
Hold our celebration first!

Ploc *runs on, to find* **Calcul** *and* **Boulot** *on the empty stage.*
Berger, **Vivette**, **Marie**, *and the* **Investors** *and*
Entertainers *follow them.*

Baron
Oh! Monsieur Ploc!

All
He's back!

Ploc
Back to face black disgrace!
If things are as I fear,
Which is how they appear,
This lady underwent exposure
To indecent assault by this composer!
I found them here!

Others
He found them here!

Ploc
Where will it end?

Others
Where will it end?

Ploc
An employee!
Where will it end? Where will it end?

Baron
What's it portend?

Calcul, **Count** *and* **Both Gonfleurs**
Is it a trend?

Others
Where will it end?

Ploc
Where will it end? Where will it end?

Boulot *steps forward and raises his arms for silence to answer.*

But **Vivette** *continues.*

Vivette
And will it end, and should it end, and must it end at all?

Boulot *raises his arms again. But* **Berger** *continues, as if* **Boulot***'s conducting had brought him in.*

Berger
Ah . . . !

Boulot *waves his arms about to demonstrate he is not conducting, but everyone picks up imaginary instruments and responds as if he* is *conducting.*

Baron (*like a double bass*)
Blum blum blum . . .

Count (*like a cello*)
Pling pling pling . . .

Froufrou *and* **Marie** (*like trumpets*)
Ta ra ra . . .

Edmond (*like a trombone*)
Ta ra ra . . .

Calcul (*like tympani*)
Boom boom boom . . .

Jules (*like bass drum*)
Thomp thomp thomp . . .

Vivette (*like clarinet*)
Ba ba ba . . .

All Instrumentalists
Where will it end?

Others (*to* **Ploc**)
You should have shown a little forethought,
Because it's very slightly *your* fault!

Ploc
What? Slightly *my* fault?

Others
Yes! Partly *your* fault!

Froufrou *and* **Sopranos**
Yes! Mostly *your* fault!

Others
Totally *your* fault!

Ploc   What? *My* fault?

Vivette
A man will stay
Some time away,
And then his thoughts will homeward bend.
Good sense and breeding
Will urge proceeding
To write and warn his lady-friend.
Then she can bake
His favourite cake,
And lay out his old familiar socks.
And by this plan
A thoughtful man,
A tactful man,
A careful man,
Can save himself from nasty shocks.

Others
And by this plan
A thoughtful man,
Can save himself from nasty shocks.
He'll eat his cake,
And then he'll make
A beeline for his dear old socks.

Vivette *and* **Others**
And by this plan
A thoughtful man,
A tactful man,
A careful man,

Can save himself from nasty shocks.

Vivette

But if a man
From some far land
Arrives home unannounced instead,
Hot-water bottle
May not be what he'll
Find warming up his longed-for bed.
His heart will ache
To have no cake.
He may find some unfamiliar socks.
Without a plan
A thoughtless man,
A tactless man,
A careless man,
Can give himself some nasty shocks.

Others

Without a plan
A thoughtless man,
Can give himself some nasty shocks.
He'll miss his cake,
And he may take
Exception to the choice of socks.

Vivette *and* **Others**

Without a plan
A thoughtless man,
A tactless man,
A careless man,
Can give himself some nasty shocks.

Ploc

Yes, yes – but one of us must go!
As you know
I'm the main investor in the show!

Baron

Quite right! You are! That being so . . .
(*To* **Berger**.) Vile seducer! Out you go!

Ploc

And I have found a star –
The biggest tenor yet –
And a proper opera
For him to do!
A tale of fire and flood,
And horns and swords and blood!
So that's the end of you!
Get out! You're through!

Berger

We scorn your gilt commercial palace!
We'll sing our songs where walls of gold do not
confine!
We'll sing them in the streets and alleys, the streets
and alleys!

Others

Out, out! This is where we have to draw the line!
Don't darken our doors again, you fearful swine!

Vivette

Go, love, and know
You will always be mine!
Know, love, as you go,
You will always be mine!

She waltzes with him.

The song we've begun,
Be it joy or be it sorrow,
Will one day be sung –
If not now, why, then, tomorrow.

Ploc *advances on them threateningly.* **Froufrou** *whirls him tactfully off into a waltz. Everyone joins in.*

Others

A song, once begun,
Be it joy or be it sorrow,
Will one day be sung –
Why not wait, why not wait until tomorrow?

Berger

> Now that we have started,
> We'll sing our song!
> Even if we're parted
> Our song will go on!
>
> Never mind the weather –
> It won't last for long.
> Soon we'll be together,
> Singing our song!

Others

> Get out! Get out!

Berger

> Even the worst weather ...

Others

> Get out! Get out!

Berger

> Never lasts for long!

Others

> Get out! Get out! Go!

Vivette *and* **Berger**

> The song we've begun, *etc.*

Others

> Better, better, better,
> Be a man and go!
> Or get a, get a, get a, get a,
> Dozen guns or so!

Berger

> Don't tell *me*, don't tell *me* that I'd
> Better, better, better
> Better be a man and go!
> No, no, no! You'd far
> Better, better, better,
> Never tell me that I'd
> Better, better, better,

Better go!
The song we've begun, *etc.*

Others

A song, once begun, *etc.*
Better not wait until tomorrow!

Berger

So, love, you know
You are mine!

Vivette

So off you go!

Berger

So . . .
I'll go!

Others

So off you go
Like a man!
So off you go!

Berger *goes.* **Vivette** *swoons gracefully away into the arms of* **Boulot**.

Curtain.

Act Three

The boulevard at night, with a patrolling gendarme, and a crowd
of people intent upon an evening out, among them the **Baron**, *the*
Gonfleur Brothers, *and the* **Count**.

All

Hats on! Step out! Let's eat!
Let's drink! Let's dance!

Tenors *and* **Baritones**

Let's go!

Sopranos

Oh, yes, let's get out and let's get going!

Tenors *and* **Baritones**

You've got a girl!

Sopranos

You've got a bloke who's in the money!

Tenors *and* **Baritones**

A pretty girl!

Sopranos

With any luck he's in the money!

Tenors *and* **Baritones**

Give life a whirl!

Sopranos

So get our fingers in the honey!

Tenors *and* **Baritones**

Let's go, let's go!
Bright lights! Night air!
Here's me! Here's you!

All

So – let's drink! Let's dance!
Come on – off we go!
Hats on! Step out! Let's eat!

Let's drink! Let's dance!
Let's live! Let's go!

Tenors *and* **Baritones**
Don't know what we want, but anyhow . . .

All
We want it now!

Tenors *and* **Baritones**
So find it fast, no matter how!

All
We want it now!
The night is only beginning!
Let's keep this old world busy spinning!
Have fun! Have more!
More! More and more!
More! More!

They arrive in front of the theatre. The billing on the marquee is for **Vivette** *and* **Arturo Poggiatura**, *in* The Horn of the Norns.

All
What's this? New show!
It's her! And him! Let's go!
So come on – the night is beginning!
Now we know how
We'll start right now!
And we'll keep the world dizzy spinning!
So in we go and off we go!
Now that we know
Where we can go,
Now that we know
Somewhere to go!
Come on! Let's go!

The crowd crams into the theatre. **Calcul** *and* **Ploc** *emerge from it and push their way in the opposite direction.*

Calcul (*anxiously*)   This famous tenor of yours – he will be here?

Ploc   Signor Poggiatura? Any minute! He's on the seven o'clock train from Milan!

Calcul *looks at his watch.*

Calcul   It's the first night!

Ploc   No need to fret. I have everything under control!

Calcul   He does know Monsieur Wagner's opera?

Ploc   *The Horn of the Norns?* He's sung it in five different cities!

They arrive at the stage door. It is guarded by a **Gendarme**.

Gendarme *(touches his képi)*   Messieurs . . .

Calcul *(alarmed)*   A gendarme? What's this?

Ploc   Just in case Monsieur Berger tries to make trouble. *(To* **Gendarme**.*)* You know what Monsieur Berger looks like?

Gendarme *(fingers his moustache)*   Clean-shaven gentleman, I believe?

Ploc   Yes, but he may attempt to disguise his appearance.

Gendarme   As long as I stand here, Monsieur, you may be sure he won't get past me!

Ploc *(to* **Calcul**)   You see? Business-like! That's what we businessmen are!

Enter **Signor Poggiatura**, *a large Italian tenor, surrounded by* **Bodyguards** *and screaming* **Fans**.

Fans   Arturo! Arturo!

Gendarme
Are you Signor Poggiatura?
Do I recognise the face?

Poggiatura
Si, si, si, son' io!

Surtitle: 'Yes, yes, 'tis I!'

Fans *and* **Bodyguards**
Yes, yes, yes, it's him!

Poggiatura
Si, si, si, si, si, si, si, si . . . !

Surtitle: 'Yes, yes, yes, yes, yes, yes, yes, yes . . .'

Poggiatura
Son' . . .

Surtitle: ''Tis . . .'

Poggiatura
. . . Io!

Surtitle: I!

Gendarme
If that's the case . . .
I'm charging you with loitering with intent to sing,
Thereby causing a nuisance in a public place.

Fans *and* **Bodyguards**
We protest! It's an outrage and a public disgrace!

The **Gendarme** *leads* **Poggiatura** *off. The* **Fans** *scream.*

Poggiatura (*speaking*)   Mi tolga le mani di dosso!

Surtitle: 'Take your hands off me!'

Poggiatura   Che significa tutto cio?

Surtitle: 'What is the meaning of this?'

Poggiatura   E una vergogna!

Surtitle: 'This is an outrage!'

Poggiatura   Mi rivolgerò al mio avvocato!

Surtitle: 'I demand to see a lawyer!'

Inside the theatre, backstage. The confused sounds to be heard before an opera, and more specifically, an opera by Wagner.

Calcul   *The Horn of the Norns* . . . It's not what people are expecting!

Ploc   But when they hear it sung by Signor Poggiatura! And Vivette . . .

Enter **Marie**, *in agitation.*

Marie   Monsieur . . . !

Calcul   What is it, Marie?

Marie   It's Madame. She's very upset. Where is he? she says. This Italian gentleman. Is he coming or isn't he? If not, she says, I might as well give up the stage now and have done with it.

Calcul   I knew it! She won't sing!

Ploc   Of course she'll sing! (*To* **Marie**.) Of course he's coming! (*To* **Calcul**.) Leave Vivette to me. I know how to handle Vivette! (*To* **Marie**.) I told her – he's on the seven o'clock train from Milan . . . !

Exeunt **Ploc** *and* **Marie**. *Enter* **Froufrou**, **Loulou** *and* **Zouzou**, *dressed as the three Norns, and carrying a horn.*

Froufrou   Monsieur! Monsieur!

Calcul (*panic-stricken*)   What is it?

Froufrou   The Horn!

Calcul   And who are you?

Froufrou   The Norns!

Calcul   Oh, yes. Signor Poggiatura? Is he here?

Loulou   No!

Zouzou   It's terrible!

Froufrou   It's the sisters!

Calcul   Whose sisters? His sisters?

Loulou   No! From the retreat!

Calcul   What are you talking about?

Enter a **Nun** *wearing a moustache, with two companions.*

Zouzou   Them!

Froufrou   Excuse me, sister . . .

She removes the moustache.

A smut on her face . . .

Nun
Is Signor Poggiatura
He whom you so keenly seek?

Others
He's the one we seek!

Nun
The flesh is weak!
He stole another's role, and, tortured by remorse,
Has withdrawn from this wicked world and
entered a retreat.

Others
Has withdrawn from this wicked world and
entered a retreat!

Calcul (*speaking*)   I knew it! I knew it!

All (*speaking*)   What are we going to do?

Calcul (*sings*)
Find someone else! But quick!

Others
Who?

Calcul
Surely somewhere at hand there must somehow be
someone!

Froufrou
Why not get from the nun some
Advice on what to do?

Calcul
How could she have a clue?

Loulou
She may know someone in a choir!

Zouzou
Maybe an easy-going friar!

All
A monk who longs to have a go!

Calcul
Hold on, hold on! I think I know!

They hurry on to the stage, set for The Horn of the Norns.

Froufrou
Us girls have all rehearsed our dance!

Loulou *and* **Zouzou**
So we can show our legs! This opera's our big
chance!

Calcul
We have our substitute right here!

Others
We have our substitute right where?

Calcul
He knows the part, so have no fear.

He drags **Boulot** *out of the prompt corner.*

Others
This is our substitute right here?

Calcul (*to* **Boulot**)   You're going on for Poggiatura. (*To
the* **Others**.) Get him dressed! Here she comes!

He bundles **Boulot** *and the* **Others** *away upstage. Enter*

Vivette, **Ploc** *and* **Marie**.

Vivette

All this fuss! I still can't understand it!
We rehearsed! Some verses from a song!
Yes! Nothing more! Even if we had planned it!
You know that! Because you came along!
If that sample made you so furious,
Why then, you may be riding for a fall!
I may start to grow rather curious,
Yes, I may become very curious
How loud you'd shout
If I sang out
And sang it all!
How loud you'd shout
If next time I performed it all!
How loud you'd shout
If I sang out
And I performed it all!
To the end!
Every note!
Every bar!
Sang it all!

Boulot *is brought forward, dressed as a Wagnerian hero. His helmet falls over his eyes.*

Ploc (*to* **Boulot**)   Signor Poggiatura! This is indeed an honour . . . !

Calcul (*lifts* **Boulot**'s *helmet*)   Monsieur Boulot.

Vivette   Monsieur Boulot?

Calcul   He'll be singing in place of Signor Poggiatura . . .

Ploc   What? Where? Why? How?

Nun

Must I repeat?
Weighed down by sin, your tenor's entered a retreat,

And expects that his penance will take at least a week.

Others
And expects that his penance will take at least a week.

Vivette (*speaking*)   And I'm to sing with Monsieur
  Boulot?

Calcul   His voice has been much admired.

Vivette   No!

Calcul   But . . .

Vivette (*sings*)
  No!

Calcul (*speaking*)   Please . . . !

Vivette
  No!

Calcul   No?

Vivette
  No! No, no, no, no! No, no, no, no, no, no, no . . . !

Ploc   So what are you saying?

Vivette
  NO!
  This is mad! I managed to resist him!
  So why make such a song and dance?
  Why? Like a fool I never even kissed him.
  You came back – and bang went our chance!
  If a song has made you so furious
  That you would wreck this show beyond recall
  I confess I've grown rather curious
  Yes, I've grown exceedingly curious,
  About your views
  Now I refuse
  To sing at all!
  Yes, that's the news
  That now I won't perform at all!
  Let's have your views

About the news
That I refuse
To sing a song at all!
Not a line!
Not a note!
Not a squeak!
Not at all!

Ploc
But you *will* sing!

Helen
I *won't*!

Calcul
If you *don't* . . .

Calcul *and* **Ploc**
Then we'll sue you!

Vivette
Then go ahead and sue!
I'll wait and hear the case!

She sits down and folds her arms.

Ploc
Oh, so that trumps our ace.

Calcul
We'll have to cancel straight away!

Ploc
Refund in full! So who will pay?

Calcul
And *I'm* the one who has to say?

He looks fearfully at the audience.

Ploc
Tell them to come another day!

Froufrou
But look, if none of us performs . . .

Froufrou, **Loulou** *and* **Zouzou**
>We'll miss our only chance
>To play the part of Norns!

Nun
>Your only hope now is to pray!

Others
>Down on our knees and pray away!

Everyone except the **Nun** *kneels and prays.*

Nun
>Lord, send us back Monsieur Berger!

Others
>Lord, send us back Monsieur Berger!
>And, please, Lord, send him back today!

The **Nun** *begins to take off her habit, and reveal herself as*
Berger.

Berger
>The song we've begun,
>Be it joy or be it sorrow,
>Will one day be sung –
>So why wait until tomorrow?

Others
>A song, once begun,
>Be it joy or be it sorrow,
>Will one day be sung –
>So why wait until tomorrow?

Vivette
>Now that we have started,
>We'll sing our song!
>We're no longer parted –
>Our song can go on!

Berger *and* **Vivette**
>Brighter-looking weather –
>The stormclouds have gone.

Here we are together,
Here we are together,
Singing, singing, singing our song!

All *except* **Ploc**
Brighter-looking weather –
The stormclouds have gone!
Here they are together,
Here they are together,
Singing, singing, singing their song!

Ploc *snatches up the great sword that* **Boulot** *was armed with.*

Ploc
Out, out! Out, out!

Others
No, no! No, no!

Ploc
I'd sooner lose money!

Others
No, no! No, no!

Ploc
Sooner lose the lot!

Others
No, no!

Ploc
Go!

Others
No!

Ploc *pursues* **Berger** *off right with the sword.* **Vivette**
runs off left, followed by **Marie**.

Calcul (*speaking*)   Come back! Come back!

Calcul *runs back and forth between the two, then upstage to look
at the audience.*

Look at them! They won't wait much longer! There's going to be a riot! They're going to set fire to the theatre!

Theatregoers
Come on!

Calcul   Listen to them! They're shouting!

Theatregoers
Let's go!

Enter from the audience the **Baron**, *the* **Count**, *and the* **Gonfleur Brothers**.

Baron   What's happening?

Calcul (*controls his panic*)   Nothing. A slight delay. A few technical problems.

Baron, **Count**, **Gonfleurs** *and* **Theatregoers**
What's up?

M. Calcul *and the three* **Entertainers** *all try to explain simultaneously*.

Baron, **Count**, **Gonfleurs** *and* **Theatregoers**
What? What?

Baron, **Count**, **Gonfleurs**
Did what?

Theatregoers
What? What?

Baron, **Count**, **Gonfleurs**
What? What?

Theatregoers
What? What?

Count
It's all obscurer and obscurer!

Theatregoers
What's up? What's wrong?

Gonfleurs
It's madness pure, and getting purer!

Theatregoers
What's going on?

Baron
Our shares are looking insecurer!

Theatregoers
What's up? What's wrong?

Baron, **Count**, **Gonfleurs**
And where is Signor Poggiatura?

Theatregoers
What's going on?
We are growing old and grey!

Baron, **Count**, **Gonfleurs** *and* **Theatregoers**
So no more delay!
Let's get under way!
Come on!

Calcul (*speaking*)   If you want a fuller explanation of events, gentlemen . . .

Baron, **Count**, **Gonfleurs** *and* **Theatregoers**
Let's go!

Berger *chases* **Ploc** *on, right, and off, left.*

Baron, **Count**, **Gonfleurs** *and* **Theatregoers**
What's up?

Froufrou (*indicates the departing* **Ploc** *and* **Berger**)   Ask *them*!

Baron, **Count**, **Gonfleurs** *and* **Theatregoers**
What? What?

Calcul, **Froufrou**, **Loulou** *and* **Zouzou**   Ask *them*!

Baron, **Count**, **Gonfleurs** *and* **Theatregoers**
What's up? What's wrong? Come on!

Theatregoers
Are you going to perform the show?

Baron, **Count**, **Gonfleurs** *and* **Theatregoers**
Say! Yes or no?

Theatregoers
If you are then kindly tell us so!

Baron, **Count**, **Gonfleurs** *and* **Theatregoers**
If not, we'll go!
The story is getting obscurer!
The madness goes on getting purer!

All *except* **Calcul** *and* **Entertainers**
Let's do the show!
Come on! Let's go!
Come on! Come on!
Let's go!

Froufrou   Quick, then! After them!

Loulou   Catch them!

Zouzou   Stop them!

Froufrou   Talk to them!

Berger *runs on from the right. At the sight of the* **Investors** *he stops.*

Calcul (*indicates* **Berger**)   There it is! Your last hope of saving your investment!

Ploc *enters right, still in pursuit.* **Berger** *dives into one of the dressing-rooms.* **Ploc** *tries to open the door, but it's locked. He mounts guard.*

Calcul   Disappearing in front of your eyes!

Count   I don't think I entirely understand.

Froufrou   *I'll* tell you. Listen, it's very simple . . .
(*Sings:*)

That lucky girl, she's got a lover!
So, got what she wants? Oh, no!

She indicates **Ploc**, *who begins to soften as she explains his situation so sympathetically.*

Froufrou *and* **Others**
That lucky girl she's got a lover!
So, got what she wants? Oh, no!

Froufrou
Silly girl – she wants another!
Lover says, No, not having it! So . . .
What to do they'll never discover –
Something somewhere has to go!

Froufrou *takes* **Ploc**'s *arm and leads him away from the dressing-room door to join everyone, as they dance.* **Zouzou** *and* **Loulou** *open the dressing-room door, and* **Berger** *looks cautiously out.*

Froufrou
That's what makes the world go round,
The world go round the merry-go-round!
That is why the world is bound
To go around the merry-go-round!

That's what makes the world go round,
The world go round the merry-go-round!
That is why the world is bound
To merrily go . . . round and round!

Others
That's what makes the world go round,
The world go round, go round and round!
That is why the world is bound
To go, to go . . . round and round!

Berger *closes the dressing-room door as* **Ploc** *returns to guard it.* **Froufrou** *once again seduces him away from the door as she sings the next verse.*

Froufrou
Everyone is wanting something!
Oh, something they want! But what?

Froufrou *and* **Others**
Everyone is wanting something!
Oh, something they want! But what?

Froufrou
Here's the odd thing, here's the rum thing –
I can tell you what it's not!
Not the one thing, never the one thing,
Never the one thing that they've got!

Others
No!

Froufrou
No!

Everyone, including **Ploc**, *dances.* **Zouzou** *and* **Loulou** *open the dressing-room door again, and* **Berger** *emerges, dressed as a Wagnerian character, and joins the dance next to* **Ploc**.

Froufrou
That's what makes the world go round, *etc.*

Berger *leads* **Ploc** *back to the door he was guarding. He gives him a key, with which* **Ploc** *locks the door. Then he slips away into the wings, accompanied by* **Froufrou**, **Loulou**, **Zouzou**, *the* **Count**, *and the* **Gonfleurs**.

Baron (*to* **Ploc**)   Monsieur, let him out! Let him sing!

Ploc *raises the sword to threaten them. They shrink back.*

Baron (*to* **Ploc**)   Consider the political consequences if this enterprise of ours is allowed to fail! The whole future of France is at stake!

Calcul   The whole future of France!

Baron
There comes a time when the truth is better,
So I'll be absolutely frank:

If you pursue your personal vendetta . . .

[**Calcul** (*at the same time*)
Make me a debtor . . .]

Baron
. . . and bankrupt his theatre . . .

[**Calcul**
. . . and bankrupt my theatre . . .]

Baron
You'll start a run upon the bank.
You'll cause the failure of the bank.

Calcul
The shock of this would be volcanic . . .

Baron
Complete financial panic!

Calcul
All of this and more,
If you won't unlock that door!

Ploc
Yes, but why are you telling *me* that?
Why not make *him* try to see that?

Calcul
Because if you make the market unsteady,
The whole of France will pay the price!

[**Baron**
Because if you make the market unsteady,
The whole of France will pay the price!]

All three
To save the nation we are surely ready,
To make a sacrifice!
A sacrifice!

Calcul

You may bring the Government down!
The mob will take over the town!

Baron

A revolution then can be expected –
Goodbye to liberty and laws!
We'll see the guillotine erected!

Calcul

The fearful guillotine erected!
The first head tumbling from its jaws
May very possibly be yours!

Baron

And you must have your head about you!
How can we face the future without you?

Look at the simple trusting creatures!
All of their hopes are fixed on you!
Every uplifted face beseeches!
Don't let catastrophe ensue!
We need a businessman to teach us
What we ought to aspire to do!

Take the key,
Set him free!
Rise above your petty jealousy!
Take the key,
Set him free!
Pave the way to immortality!

I see the Emperor commending
Your mighty magnanimity.
I see the humble Ploc soon ending
Up as a Baron just like me!
The noble line of Ploc extending
All the way to eternity!

Baron *and* **Calcul**

Take the key,
Set him free!

Rise above your petty jealousy!
Take the key,
Set him free!
Pave the way to immortality!

[**Ploc**
Take the key,
Set him free?
Rise above my petty jealousy?
Take the key,
Set him free?
Pave the way to immortality?]

Calcul
So choose your future state . . .

Baron
Choose which will be your fate . . .

Calcul
To be a Lord,
With coat of arms . . .

Baron *and* **Calcul**
A Lord with arms, or else instead
A commoner without a head!

Ploc *stands with his eyes closed.*

Baron
Is he sleeping?

Calcul
No, he's blinking.

Baron
He's praying. Or weeping.

[**Calcul**
He's praying. Or weeping.]

Ploc
I'm thinking.

Calcul

Then think once, think twice – we are offering the
    chance,
A chance you should not lightly cast aside,
To get all the credit for saving France –
And all you have to do is swallow your pride!

Ploc

I thank you but I'd sooner swallow the key!

[**Baron**

He'd sooner swallow the key!]

Ploc

And give France the credit for saving me!

[**Baron**

Credit for same!]

Baron *and* **Calcul**

Come! A chance you should not lightly cast aside
And all you have to do is swallow your pride!

[**Ploc**

A chance that I can lightly cast aside
Though all I have to do is swallow my pride!]

Ploc

No need – I have my own solution
To the problem of saving France.
Here's how I'll ward off revolution –
Go on myself and do a dance,
Perform a little song and dance!

Baron

He is bent on confrontation!

Baron *and* **Calcul**

He is seeking obliteration!
Cataclysmic annihilation!

The **Audience** *begin to climb out of the boxes as a revolutionary mob. The lights fade to flickering red torchlight.*

Baron *and* **Calcul**

Woe! Woe, woe, woe, woe, woe!

He's thought once, thought twice, and rejected the
chance,

Decided quite lightly to cast it aside!

And out of the foundering wreck of France,

The one thing he saves is his pride!

The sole survivor is his pride!

Everything gone but Ploc's own pride!

[Ploc

Oh! Oh, oh, oh, oh, oh!

I've thought once, thought twice, and rejected the
chance,

Decided quite lightly to cast it aside!

And out of the foundering wreck of France,

The one thing I save is my pride!

The sole survivor is my pride!

Everything gone but Ploc's own pride!]

Ploc *is left spotlit, with sword held defiantly aloft like a cross,
amidst the collapse of civilisation as we know it. Enter*
Froufrou, **Loulou** *and* **Zouzou**.

Froufrou   Signor Poggiatura! He's arrived!

Others   Signor Poggiatura?

*Pause. The lights come up. The revolutionary mob climbs back
into the boxes.* **Ploc** *slowly lowers his sword. Enter the* **Count**
and the **Gonfleurs**.

All

Can it *be* him?

Shall we see him,

Actually here,

Thrillingly near?

Enter **Bodyguards**, *a* **Doctor**, *and a* **Chef**.

Everyone sighing,

Grown men crying!

Probably soon
Ladies will swoon.

Though we are not clear
How he got here,
Now he is,
We all are his!

Who minds his lateness?
Hail his greatness!
Say Hurray,
He's come today!

Enter **Signor Poggiatura**. *He is even larger than at his appearance earlier. But somehow he looks more like* **Berger** *than the original did.*

All
Oh, he's here now!
Large and clear now!
Feast your eyes –
What a size!

Oh, he's here!
Large and clear now!
Yes, he's here!

Berger/Poggiatura My friends . . . ! My friends . . . !

Baron Welcome, signore! Welcome!

Calcul You can't imagine how much this means to us all!

Berger/Poggiatura Is nothing.

Others
Lift up that voice of yours and sway us!
Rule our hearts, command us like a king!
Sweetly impose order on chaos!
Go forth and sing!

Berger/Poggiatura But first I say one word. This production. What is the Konzept?

Others The Konzept!

Berger/Poggiatura   I tell you what is the Konzept.
(*Sings:*)

I notice that you all are looking grim and gruff.
It's true the saga of the Norns is grisly stuff.
They led a fairly gruesome life, those fatal hags,
High up among the frozen waste of alpine crags.
But, just like everyone,
They loved a spot of fun!

Others
So Norns, like everyone,
Were not averse to fun?

Berger/Poggiatura
Ah! They had fun
Lots of fun!
They had fun
By the ton!

Others
They had fun
Lots of fun!
They had fun
By the ton!

Berger/Poggiatura
Drank a jug,
In the snug!
Had a hug!
Cut a rug!

Others
Drank a jug,
In the snug!
Had a hug!
Cut a rug!

Berger/Poggiatura
La-lai-too-la la la la la!
Oh, they yodel-ai-yodelled all night and all day,
Till their cares had been yodel-ai-yodelled away!

Others
Yodel-aee! Yodel-aee!

Berger/Poggiatura
Tra la la la la!

Others
Tra la la la la!

All
So come,
Everyone!
We'll have fun,
Lots of fun!

Yes, come,
Everyone!
We'll have fun,
Everyone!

Berger/Poggiatura
They wove the tangled fabric of tormented lives,
Made husbands into mincemeat and then roasted
    wives.
The nature of the job would give the normal Norn
By any usual standards ample cause to mourn.
But no! They were as gay
As cuckoo-clocks in May!

Chorus
Up there among the rocks?
As gay as cuckoo-clocks?

Berger/Poggiatura
Ah! They had fun *etc*.

Enter **Marie**.

Marie   She's coming! She's coming!

All *except* **Ploc** *and* **Berger/Poggiatura**
Will she sing with this one?
Maybe yes, maybe no.

What, could she dismiss one
Last chance for the show?

If she can't have that one,
Will she stay? Will she go?
She must like the fat one!
Who knows? Touch and go!

Enter **Vivette**, *in Wagnerian costume.*

Vivette
I heard a voice that I was certain,
Sweetly certain that I knew.

Ploc
Yes, look, he's here – you do, you do!
Signor Poggiatura from La Scala!
So, overture and curtain!
And let's get under way!

Froufrou *and* **Others**
Quickly, no more delay!

Vivette
A big star, so I heard.
Yes, but this! No – absurd!

Berger/Poggiatura
May I have a word?

Froufrou
Explain what sort of man you are!

Baron *and* **Calcul**
And use your massive charms...

Baron, **Calcul** *and* **Others**
... to overwhelm her qualms.

Berger/Poggiatura
I think that I can state
My words will carry weight.
(*To* **Vivette**.) You'll find the music is familiar –
It's a story that you know.

And there's a song a simple shepherd
Sang to a goddess long ago.

Vivette
And made far too much of her beauty!

Ploc
Enough, enough! Do as I say!

Baron *and* **Calcul**
Your contract clearly states your duty!

Vivette
The contract speaks – I obey!

Count, **Gonfleurs**, **Baron** *and* **Calcul**
We're there! We have cracked it!
Set fair now to act it!
We're there! We're there! We're there!
We're there! There!

Berger/Poggiatura
So we unfold
The story of life!

He reveals himself to be **Berger**, *dressed as Paris. At the same time* **Vivette** *throws off her cloak and helmet, to reveal her costume as Helen and her long blonde hair.*

Berger
A man is bold,
And wins a wife!

As they sing, the lights go down, until only **Berger** *and* **Vivette** *are left in the spotlight. They climb into a gondola.*

Berger *and* **Vivette**
Yes!

Berger
Two people singing . . .

Vivette
Two people singing . . .

Both
Singing a sweet and simple song.

Berger
Lovers have sung it . . .

Vivette
Lovers have sung it . . .

Both
Since the world was young.

Vivette
Soon the notes fade . . .

Berger
Soon the notes fade . . .

Both
Soon the notes fade, and life moves on!

Berger
Sing it!

Vivette
Sing it!

Berger
Sing it!

Vivette
Sing it!
And sing till the song has been sung.

Berger
And sing till the song has been sung.

All
Ah!

Women
A song, a song, an old sweet song!

Men
A song, a song, an old sweet song!

Women
A song, a song, an old sweet song!

Men
A song, a song, an old sweet song!

Women
Two people singing!

Men
Two people singing!

All
Singing a sweet and simple song!

Men
Two people singing!

Women
Two people singing!

Men *and* **Women**
They'll sing their song!
Oh, while they have breath to sing,
They'll sing, they'll sing their song!

Vivette *and* **Berger**
We'll sing our song!
Oh, while we have breath to sing,
We'll sing, we'll sing our song!

The gondola that **Berger** *and* **Helen** *are in begins to rise into the air. It is hanging beneath a balloon.*

All   A balloon?

Calcul   You're flying?

Ploc   Where are you off to?

Berger   Home!

Berger *begins to take off his Paris costume.*

Berger
One more surprise

As I begin
To cast aside
My last disguise!
I am . . .

He reveals a uniform tunic covered in medals.

Prince Leopold von Hohenzollern-Sigmaringen, from
. . . Berlin!

All *except* **Berger** *and* **Vivette**
What?

Count
Chap out of Prussia, primitive Prussia, halfway to
Russia!

Count, **Baron**, **Gonfleurs** *and* **Ploc**
Took us for a ride!

Chorus
He lied and lied and lied!

Gonfleurs
He's some Hun flying for Prussia, prying for Prussia,
spying for Prussia!

Count, **Baron**, **Gonfleurs** *and* **Ploc**
He should be inside!

Chorus
He spied and spied and spied!

Ploc
I tried hard to warn you all,
I tried and tried and tried!

Baron
And now he's going to rush her over to Prussia –
meaning to usher
In the bitter end of all our national pride!

Count, **Baron**, **Gonfleurs** *and* **Ploc**
Can we endure it? Can we endure it? Can we endure
it?

Chorus
No, no, no!

Count, **Baron**, **Gonfleurs** *and* **Ploc**
Will we endure it? Will we endure it?
Stand here and endure it?

Chorus
Oh, oh, oh, oh!

Count, **Baron**, **Gonfleurs** *and* **Ploc**
Will we endure it? Will we endure it?

All *except* **Berger** *and* **Vivette**
No, no, no, no, no, no!

Chorus
So, so, how do we cure it? How do we cure it? How
do we cure it?

Count, **Baron**, **Gonfleurs** *and* **Ploc**
Here's how we can cure it! No need to endure it!
We know one way to cure it!
Time to play the part
We've been waiting for –
What a perfect chance to start
The Franco-Prussian war!

All
We'll close the score
With a major war!
With the Franco-Prussian war!

The balloon vanishes into the sky. Everyone pursues it off.
Enter, running after them, the real **Signor Poggiatura**,
wearing only his underclothes, shaking his fist.

Curtain.